HM

CONSPIRACY AND CIVIL LIBERTIES

A Memorandum submitted to the Law Commission by the Cobden Trust and the National Council for Civil Liberties

ROBERT HAZELL

OCCASIONAL PAPERS ON SOCIAL ADMINISTRATION NO. 55
Editorial Committee under the Chairmanship of Professor Brian Abel-Smith
Published by G. Bell & Sons, York House, Portugal Street, London, W.C.2

First published 1974

ISBN 07135 1909 6

MADE AND PRINTED IN ENGLAND BY
WILLMER BROTHERS LIMITED
BIRKENHEAD

FOREWORD

The series of *Occasional Papers* was started in 1960 to supply the need for a medium of publication for studies in the field of social policy and administration which fell between the two extremes of the short article and the full-length book. Since the inception of this Series of papers, it has, however, been extended to include many which might better be described as books: comparative speed of publication being one factor that has attracted authors to us. It was thought that such a series would not only meet a need among research workers and writers concerned with contemporary social issues, but would also strengthen links between students of the subject and administrators, social workers, committee members and others with responsibilities and interest in the social services.

Contributions are welcome from any source and should be submitted in the first instance to the Secretary, The Social Administration Research Trust, at the London School of Economics. A list of some of the earlier papers which are still available is printed on the back of this volume. Copies may be obtained through any bookseller.

Brian Abel-Smith
Chairman, Social Administration Research Trust

THE AUTHOR

Robert Hazell was educated as a Scholar at Eton and at Wadham College, Oxford, where he took degrees in Politics, Philosophy & Economics and then in Law. He is now a Barrister.

PREFACE

All credit for the idea behind this book must go to Christine Jackson, the Secretary of the Cobden Trust. In 1972 because of mounting concern at the increasing use of conspiracy charges the Trust (which is the research branch of the National Council for Civil Liberties) decided to submit evidence to the Law Commission on the reform of the law, and I was asked to prepare that evidence. Our memorandum was sent to the Law Commission in February 1973, and this book is almost identical to that memorandum, with the addition only of new material (principally the decision of the House of Lords in *Kamara v. D.P.P.*) which emerged between January and July 1973.

In preparing this study I have received every cooperation from the Cobden Trust, and I owe a particular debt to Christine Jackson and Larry Grant for their constant encouragement and criticism, and to Catherine Scorer and Enid Sheward who typed successive versions of the manuscript. Special thanks are also due to James Munby, who devised the classification of the different heads of conspiracy which appears at the end of Chapter 3. Graham Zellick and Alan Paterson gave me their comments on the first draft, and Michael Sherrard, Q.C., Bernard Simons and M. Pierre Lavirotte all discussed small sections of it with me; and in Oxford I benefited greatly from conversations with Professor Sir Rupert Cross, Dr Ian Brownlie and Tsatsu Tsikata. I should also like to acknowledge the cooperation of the Director of Public Prosecutions, who gave me information on recent prosecutions for conspiracy to effect a public mischief. And finally I should like to thank Bo and Bebe Jones, with whom I stayed in Harvard whilst revising this book in July 1973.

Since that revision the Law Commission has itself published its own criticisms and proposals for the reform of the law of conspiracy, which are substantially the same as my own. I have not been able to incorporate any references to the Law Commission's Working Paper, but I would like to take this opportunity to welcome their proposals, and to express the earnest hope that the Government will implement their main recommendation, that conspiracy be restricted to agreements to commit a crime, as soon as possible.

November 1973 ROBERT HAZELL

TO MY PARENTS

CONTENTS

1. INTRODUCTION

'The use of the conspiracy charge has been criticised so often and for so many years that it would no doubt have been abolished long ago unless there were some real merit left in it.'[1] (Lord Widgery in the House of Lords, 24 July 1972)

Only two books have been published on the English law of criminal conspiracy, one in 1873[2] and one in 1924.[3] Both of them subjected conspiracy to harsh criticism; but in 1973, 100 years after Wright's book and 50 years after Harrison's, the conspiracy charge is if anything more widesweeping than ever. The publication of books on the subject does not appear to be a powerful vehicle of reform. But recently general dissatisfaction with the law led to conspiracy being made the subject of a reference to the Law Commission; and this is a far more hopeful development because it does at last raise the possibility of real change.

Reform is now a matter of urgent necessity, because the conspiracy charge represents one of the greatest threats to civil liberties in English criminal law. It empowers the police to charge people with offences which, if committed by a single person, would not be a crime.[4] It empowers the police to charge people with offences which, if committed by a single person, would not be a crime.[4] It enables the prosecuting authorities to bypass the statutory safeguards laid down by Parliament for prosecutions in certain classes of cases.[5] It gives to prosecuting counsel the advantage of a much more favourable procedure at the trial.[6] It requires the judge in certain kinds of case virtually to make up the law as he goes along.[6a] And it allows the courts to hand down sentences in excess of the statutory maxima authorised by Parliament for the substantive offence.[7]

[1] Hansard, House of Lords 24 July 1972 col. 118.
[2] Wright: *The Law of Criminal Conspiracies and Agreements.*
[3] Harrison: *Conspiracy as a Crime and as a Tort.*
[4] E.g. *Kamara* 1972 3 All ER 999.
[5] In particular prosecutions under the Obscene Publications Act. See chapter 4, pages 61–4.
[6] See chapter 5.
[6a] Particularly in prosecutions for conspiracy to effect a public mischief, where what is a public mischief is a question of law for the judge. But this also applies to a considerable extent to the public morals and public decency cases, and to prosecutions for conspiracy to commit a tort.
[7] See chapter 7.

As if this were not enough, the conspiracy weapon, to judge by reported cases, is being used more than it ever has been before. This may simply be a result of the great increase in criminal cases generally; but even a proportionate increase is undesirable because of the procedural laxity in conspiracy trials mentioned above. What is far more disturbing is the use of the conspiracy weapon in controversial cases like the trials of Oz[8] and IT,[9] and of Peter Hain and of the African demonstrators in *Kamara*.[10] It is impossible to prove that these were political trials in the sense that the defendants were on trial for their political beliefs; but what can be said with some confidence is that the offences with which they were charged were all motivated by, and the result of, their political beliefs. What marks out these quasi-political cases from the 'ordinary' criminal case is that because of the tremendous publicity they receive, it is particularly important that justice should manifestly be seen to be done; but it is precisely in these cases that judges and juries appear to hand down decisions based on their own ideas of what is just, or what is good for society – and this role in part is forced upon them by the nature of the conspiracy charge.

Nowhere is this more evident than in the development over the past ten to fifteen years of conspiracy to corrupt public morals and conspiracy to outrage public decency – two of the charges used against Oz and IT, respectively. These charges in particular are subjected to close scrutiny in the pages which follow; as is the other charge in the 'third head' of conspiracy, conspiracy to effect a public mischief. It appears to many people that in prosecutions for these offences it is British justice itself which is on trial. The use by nineteenth-century judges of the conspiracy charge as a weapon to hinder the emergence of the trade unions has been described this century by Cyril Asquith (later a distinguished Lord Justice) as 'an impressive illustration of judicial bias'[11] and by Lord Diplock as a 'bitter legacy'.[12] Will judges in the twenty-first century make similar remarks about their predecessors' use of the conspiracy weapon to suppress the emergence of an alternative society and an alternative morality in the twentieth?

In this context much will inevitably be said about judicial legislation, and one of the criticisms levelled by lawyers at this book may well be that it adopts a naive view of how the common law works, and in particular of how it develops. It should be made quite clear at the outset that it is fully appreciated that some degree of judicial legislation is unavoidable in the development of the common law – indeed, of any legal system; but that degree should be kept to a minimum. Nor is it merely a question of degree; for judicial legislation differs funda-

[8] 1971 3 WLR 939.
[9] 1972 3 WLR 143.
[10] 1973 AC 435.
[11] *Trade Union Law for Laymen* (1927) p.14.
[12] In *Knuller* 1972 3 WLR at 168.

mentally from legislative law making. The judge is *not* free to follow his own ideas of what will maximize the social welfare; the legislature (subject to political constraints) is. Judges can only legislate where a statute is not clear, or where there is no statute; and if the gaps in the law are too wide (as it is intended here in some cases to show) then it is time for Parliament to intervene.

The most difficult part of the book to write has been the chapter on Proposals for Reform. Is there any merit left in the charge of conspiracy at all? And if so, which parts of the crime are still of use and which can safely be discarded? The quotation by Lord Widgery which heads this Introduction, although something of a *non sequitur,* is a useful starting point for this enquiry because it does conveniently raise these two main questions.

As to the first, it will not really receive a proper answer here, because it is much too large a question for the scope of this study; but it is extremely important to raise it. If conspiracy were dropped from the present trio of inchoate offences, would attempt, and incitement, and aiding and abetting provide alternative charges in most of the cases where at present the charge is conspiracy? Such a change would obviously involve a major re-drawing of the boundaries of criminal responsibility in English law; but most civil law systems manage to do without a crime of conspiracy. It is hoped that the Law Commission has considered this question in its Working Paper on Inchoate Offences – or if it has not, that it will do so in its Papers on Conspiracy. The question is unfortunately much too large for the present study because it really requires a survey of unreported cases (reported cases being almost certainly unrepresentative of the whole). Before recommending the total abolition of conspiracy one would have to find out in what sort of day-to-day cases the conspiracy charge is used, whether the charge is necessary, and what alternative charges are available. In what follows the continued existence of conspiracy in some form will of necessity be a presupposition of the whole book, since I have not gathered enough evidence to be able confidently to recommend its abolition.

With that reservation, almost every other aspect of the law of criminal conspiracy will be investigated. Civil conspiracy will not be touched upon, however, and I will not concern myself with what might be called the 'technical' rules of conspiracy – questions such as whether a defendant can be found guilty of conspiracy if all his alleged co-conspirators are acquitted,[13] or whether a husband and wife can be guilty of conspiracy.[14] The case-law on these questions provides some

[13] See *Thomson* 1965 50 Cr. App. Rep 1.
[14] See *Mawji* 1957 AC 526.

illogical and unsatisfactory answers, but they are matters of only peripheral importance, many of which can be cleared up by a 'unilateral' definition of the crime.[15] My primary concern will be to describe what the present law of conspiracy is, to show how it represents a threat to our civil liberties, and to suggest ways in which those liberties can be safeguarded.

I have attempted to state the law as it stood in July 1973.

[15] *E.g.* the definition in the American Model Penal Code, given in chapter 8 (b).

2. THE HISTORICAL BACKGROUND

> 'The offence of conspiracy is more difficult to be ascertained precisely than any other for which indictment lies; and is, indeed, rather to be considered as governed by positive decisions than by any consistent and intelligible principles of law.'[16] (Serjeant Talfourd, 1829)

The history of conspiracy has been well documented,[17] but it is necessary briefly to describe its early development partly because, as Serjeant Talfourd recognized, a few landmark decisions have greatly influenced the growth of the law (they exemplify, in Cardozo's famous words, the 'tendency of a principle to expand itself to the limit of its logic'), and partly because seventeenth and eighteenth century cases are still relied on relatively frequently by the courts.[18]

The Origins of Conspiracy

Conspiracy was originally a statutory offence, developed in the thirteenth century to prevent malicious prosecutions. The Third Ordinance of Conspirators[19] defined conspirators as 'they that do confeder or bind themselves by Oath, Covenant or other Alliance, that every of them shall aid and support the Enterprise of each other falsely and maliciously to indite, or falsely to maintain Pleas'. There was no common law generalization of this offence; and it was not complete until the person falsely accused had actually been indicted and acquitted. It was only in the seventeenth century that the crime of conspiracy found a broader application, in the hands of the Court of Star Chamber. In the words of Lord Reid,[20]

> 'It appears to be generally accepted that the offence of criminal conspiracy was the creature of the Star Chamber. So far as I am able to judge, the summary in Kenny's Outlines of Criminal Law (17th edn), s.59, is a fair one. There it is said that the criminal side of

[16] Dickinson's Practical Guide to the Quarter Sessions, 3rd Edition.
[17] See in particular Wright, *The Law of Criminal Conspiracies and Agreements* (1873); Winfield, *History of Conspiracy and Abuse of Legal Procedure* (1921); Sayre 1922 Harv. LR 393; Harrison, *Conspiracy as a Crime and as a Tort* (1924); and for an original (if slightly tendentious) analysis, Lord Diplock in *Knuller* 1972 3 WLR at 166–169 and Lord Hailsham in *Kamara* 1973 3 WLR 198.
[18] See especially, of course, *Shaw v DPP* 1962 AC 220.
[19] 33 Edw. 1.
[20] In *Shaw v DPP* 1961 2 All ER 446 at 455.

conspiracy was "emphasized by the Star Chamber, which recognised its possibilities as an engine of government and moulded it into a substantive offence of wide scope, whose attractions were such that its principles were gradually adopted by the common law courts . . ."'

The Seventeenth-Century Rule

This widening of the scope of conspiracy occurred in two stages. The first stage was provided by *The Poulterers' Case* (1611),[21] an action in civil conspiracy. There the falsely accused plaintiff was so manifestly innocent that the grand jury refused to indict him; and when he sued his accusers for damages they claimed that they could not be liable, since he had never been indicted and acquitted. The Star Chamber, however, rejected this argument by holding that the *conspiring together* constituted the essence of the offence, rather than the subsequent false indictment. From here it was an easy step to the doctrine that since the essence of the crime is the agreement, no other overt act is necessary. The conspiring together itself constitutes an act which may furnish the basis of criminal liability.

The second stage in the seventeenth-century development of conspiracy involved extending the scope of the offence from agreements to bring malicious prosecutions to agreements to commit *all* crimes, both felonies and misdemeanours. By the time that the Court of Star Chamber disappeared, and its mantle had been assumed by the Court of King's Bench, what has been called the Seventeenth Century Rule[22] was well established: a combination to commit *any* crime was a criminal conspiracy. The Seventeenth Century Rule does appear to have been limited to agreements to commit *crimes*.[22a] In *Thorp* (1697),[23] for example, an early attempt was made to extend the law by making criminal a combination to procure a marriage; but from the report the only question at issue appears to have been whether the object of the combination was to procure a criminal act – there was no suggestion that without this element the combination might still be criminal. However, in the seventeenth century the distinction between law and morals was not so closely observed as it is today, and many immoral acts were punished by the courts in their capacity as guardians of the public morals, whether they were committed by individuals or by combinations. Thus in 1664 the Court of Kings Bench told Sir Charles Sidley that 'although there was not now a Star Chamber, still they would have him know that this court is *custos morum* of all the subjects of the King'.[24] And as late as 1774 we find Lord Mansfield

[21] 9 Co Rep 55b 77 ER 813.
[22] by Wright, *op cit* p. 26.
[22a] For a contrary view see Lord Hailsham's summary in *Kamara* 1973 3 WLR 198 at 208–9.
[23] 1967 5 Mod 221.
[24] *Sidley* 1 Sid 168, 82 ER 1036.

saying[25] 'Whatever is *contra bonos mores et decorum,* the principles of our law prohibit, and the Kings Court, as the general censor and guardian of the public manners, is bound to restrain and punish'. But it is important to realize in the early conspiracy cases that when the courts punished immoral acts done in combination, they considered themselves to be punishing agreements to commit *crimes.*

Extension beyond the Seventeenth Century Rule

By the end of the eighteenth century this view had changed, and the general impression was that an agreement to commit an 'unlawful' act might be a criminal conspiracy, where 'unlawful' meant something wider than merely 'criminal'. Three factors had contributed to this further extension of the law. In the first place, there was the development of the common law misdemeanour of conspiracy to defraud. Cheats at one time had been criminal, but in the eighteenth century it was settled that a *private* cheat was not a crime, but only a civil wrong. Thus in *Jones*[26] Holt C.J. had asked, 'Shall we indict one man for making a fool of another? Let him bring his action'. However at the same time the courts expressly reserved the criminality of cheats *in combination*: an example is *Wheatley*[27] where Lord Mansfield said:

> 'The offence that is indictable must be such a one as affects the *public*. . . . For there are deceptions that common care and prudence are not sufficient to guard against. So, if there be a *conspiracy* to cheat, for ordinary care and caution is no guard against this.'

This doctrine proved very useful in the days when the offence of obtaining property by deception was inadequately developed,[28] and it is still established law[29] that a combination to defraud is a criminal conspiracy, even though the deception used would *not* be criminal if employed by one person alone.

The second factor which led to the belief that combinations could be criminal, even though formed for a purpose which was not criminal, was the case of the Brewers of London, *Starling's Case* (1663),[30] a conspiracy to lessen the King's revenue by impoverishing the farmers of the Excise. The case was probably misinterpreted (the defendants' purposes were almost certainly punishable independently of combination – see Wright, *op. cit.* p. 29), but it forms the origin of the doctrine that a conspiracy may be criminal if it is directed against the public as a whole or against the government.

[25] In *Jones v. Randall* 1774 Lofft 384 98 ER 706.
[26] 1703 2 Ld Raym 1013.
[27] 1761 2 Burr. 1127 (italics added in quotation).
[28] See now Theft Act 1968 ss 15 & 16.
[29] *E.g. Warburton* 1870 LR 1 CCR 274, 11 Cox 584; *Fountain* 1966 1 WLR 212.
[30] 1 Sid 174, 1 Keb 650.

The third factor which undermined the clear limits of the Seventeenth Century Rule was the sweeping statement by Hawkins, in his much-used *Pleas of the Crown* (1717), that 'all confederacies whatsoever, wrongfully to prejudice a third person are highly criminal at common law'.[30a] None of the seven cases cited by Hawkins in fact gives authority for this proposition;[31] but the seed was laid for a further extension of the crime.[32]

Lord Denman's definition

In the case of *Jones,*[33] in 1832, Lord Denman C.J. proffered a working definition of conspiracy which has been adopted unquestioningly by the courts ever since, and has been used for a still *further* extension of conspiracy.[34] Lord Denman said that the indictment must 'charge a *conspiracy to do an unlawful act, or a lawful act by unlawful means*'. He himself had doubts about the generality of this formula, for when in *Peck*[35] (1839) his own phrase was cited to him by counsel, he said 'I do not think the antithesis very correct', and in *King*[36] (1884) where the attempt was repeated, he clearly explained the meaning of the phrase as being a limitation and not a definition by observing 'the words "at least" should accompany that'. And in *Seward*[37] (1834) he made it quite clear what *he* understood by 'unlawful' in his formula by saying '... when it is said that such a proceeding is a conspiracy, because it is to be carried into effect by unlawful means, we must see in the means stated something which amounts to an *offence*' (italics added).

But by then it was too late: the damage had been done. 'Like the magic jingle in some fairy tale, this famous formula was seized upon by judges labouring bewildered through the conspiracy cases as a ready solution for all their difficulties. It would fit any conspiracy case whatever; it was, so to speak, ready to wear, and obviated the necessity of carefully thinking through or correctly analysing the doctrine of conspiracy.'[38] In 1868 Willes J., giving the Judges' opinion to the House of Lords in *Mulcahy,*[39] as to whether an agreement could be a sufficient overt act within the meaning of a Victorian treason statute,[40] said this (at p. 317):

'A conspiracy consists not merely in the *intention* of two or more

[30a] 8th Edn (1795) 1 PC c72, s2.
[31] Wright, Harrison and Sayre *op. cit* are all agreed on this.
[32] As late as 1954 this phrase was cited from Hawkins as 'a work of great authority' by Lord Goddard C.J. in *Newland* 1954 1 QB 158 at 166.
[33] 4 B & Ad 345.
[34] For a particularly blatant example see *Kamara* 1972 3 All ER 999 (discussed below chapter 4, pp. 51–52).
[35] 9 Ad & E 686.
[36] 1844 7 QB 782.
[37] 1 Ad & E 706.
[38] Sayre 22 Harv LR 393 at 405.
[39] LR 3 HL 306.
[40] 11 Vict c 12.

to do an unlawful act, or to do a lawful act by unlawful means. So long as such a design rests in intention only it is not indictable. When two agree to carry it into effect, the very plot is an act in itself ... punishable if for a *criminal* object or for the use of *criminal* means' (italics added).

The House of Lords approved this definition, and did so again in *Quinn v Leathem,*[41] and the Denman formula has been cited and approved in at least twenty reported conspiracy cases since Lord Denman C.J. first laid it down; and over the course of those twenty cases the word 'unlawful' has been progressively diluted in meaning. In the seventeenth century 'unlawful' had meant simply criminal; in the nineteenth century it was stretched to include not merely criminal but tortious (which was perfectly legitimate in cases of conspiracy to *defraud* – for example, *Jones* itself[42] – but not with regard to other torts); and now 'unlawful' includes a third class of acts, '... certain other acts ... which ... are not breaches of law at all, but nevertheless are outrageously immoral or else, in some way, extremely injurious to the public'.[43]

Probably the worst abuse of this loose formula is to be found in the nineteenth century industrial cases, when the judges used conspiracy to muzzle any effective action by the emergent trade unions. At the beginning of the century as a result of the Combination Acts trade unions were themselves illegal; but even after these Acts had been repealed common law conspiracy, as interpreted by the judges, ensured that almost any activity by trade unionists in the way of striking or picketing was a criminal offence. There were scores of prosecutions; only three will be mentioned here as a sample of what the judges were doing.

In *Rowlands*[44] tinplate workers who were paid below average wages and obliged to give their employer six months notice were organized in a strike by a London union. They were convicted of conspiracy to molest and obstruct their employer, because they had interfered with his 'lawful freedom of action'. In *Druitt*[45] a group of tailors was prosecuted for picketing their masters' shops in London. Their picketing had been perfectly peaceful, but Bramwell B. declared that their action was illegal as a conspiracy to molest if it included 'abusive language or gestures', or anything 'calculated to have a deterring effect on the minds of ordinary persons, by exposing them to have their motions watched and to encounter black looks'.[46] Four years later a

41 1901 AC 495.
42 4 B & Ad 345.
43 Kenny, *Outlines of Criminal Law* s457, quoted by Lord Reid in *Shaw v DPP* 1961 2 All ER 446 at 456.
44 1851 5 Cox 466.
45 1867 10 Cox 592.
46 *Ibid* at 601–2.

group of women was convicted for saying 'Bah' to blacklegs. Finally in *Bunn*[47] workers in a gasworks, who had threatened to strike unless a colleague dismissed for union activity was reinstated, were convicted of conspiracy because their combination involved 'an unjustifiable annoyance and interference with the masters in the conduct of their business ... such annoyance and interference as would be likely to have a deterring effect upon masters of ordinary nerve'.[48] The reaction of the trade unions to these decisions was one of intense anger; and eventually their persistent political pressure did result in legislation – in Disraeli's Conspiracy and Protection of Property Act 1875. Section 3 of the Act provided that no combination to do or procure any act in contemplation or furtherance of a trade dispute should be a criminal conspiracy, unless the act itself would be punishable as a crime.

So ended a century of conflict between the workers and the judiciary, and common law criminal conspiracy no longer has any place in trade disputes.[49] But the common law definition of conspiracy was not changed one iota by the legislation. The Denman formula is still the law, and the meaning of 'unlawful' is still as uncertain – possibly at the moment even more uncertain – than it ever was. In 1961 Lord Tucker said of the meaning of 'unlawful'[50]:

> 'It has for long been accepted that there are some consequences which are criminal although the acts agreed to be done are not *per se* criminal or tortious if done by individuals ... The difficulty with regard to this third class of conspiracy has always been to define its limits or give it a label which will include all its manifestations. It was referred to by Viscount Simon L.C. in *Crofter Hand Woven Harris Tweed Co. v. Veitch*[51] as one in which "the purpose aimed at, though not perhaps specifically illegal, was one which would undermine principles of commercial or moral conduct".'

We have come a long way from the clarity and simplicity of the Seventeenth Century Rule, that to be indictable a conspiracy must be an agreement to commit a crime; and the purpose of this historical introduction has been to show how the scope of conspiracy has been gradually extended by the courts. Left to themselves the judges will indeed expand a principle to the limit of its logic – and beyond. In the

[47] 1872 12 Cox 316.

[48] *Ibid* at 348–9.

[49] But after 1875 the judges decided there was still *civil* liability for conspiracy. In 1895 trade unionists who posted a 'black list' of blackleg workers were held liable in damages for conspiracy to injure; in 1892 and 1902 the circulation of lists of strikers and trouble makers by employers' associations was held *not* unlawful, because they were defending legitimate self-interest! For a recent example of an action in civil conspiracy in an industrial dispute, see *Rookes v. Barnard* 1964 AC 1129.
Nor has criminal conspiracy wholly disappeared from the sphere of industrial relations: in 1973 a number of pickets were prosecuted for intimidation under section 7 of the Conspiracy and Protection of Property Act 1875. These prosecutions are discussed in chapter 6.

[50] In *Shaw v. D.P.P.* 1961 2 All ER at 461.

[51] 1942 AC at p. 439.

nineteenth century as we have seen, the use of the conspiracy weapon to curb trade union activity had to be prevented eventually by legislation. But it is like a hydra-headed monster: by reiterated abuse of the Denman formula the judges have continued to allow conspiracy to grow, so that legislation is once again necessary. Just how wide the coverage of conspiracy now is will be examined in the next chapter.

3. THE PRESENT LAW

(a) *The 'Agreement' and Mens Rea*

Before considering what classes of conduct are now 'unlawful' we must briefly indicate what the law of conspiracy understands by an agreement, and what degree of criminal intent is required in each conspirator.

An agreement which is enforceable contractually is not necessary, but the parties must at least have reached a decision to do the unlawful act. In *Walker* (1962)[52] the appellant's conviction was quashed even though it was 'perfectly clear' that he had discussed with others the proposition of stealing a payroll, because it was not proved that they had got beyond the stage of negotiation when the appellant withdrew. But once the intention is formed and the agreement is made the crime of conspiracy is complete:

> 'The crime of conspiracy is completely committed, if it is committed at all, the moment two or more have agreed that they will do, at once or at some future time, certain things. It is not necessary in order to complete the offence that any one thing should be done beyond the agreement. The conspirators may repent and stop, may have no opportunity, or may be prevented, or may fail. Nevertheless the crime is complete: it was completed when they agreed.' (Brett J.A. in *Aspinall* 1876)[53]

In the ordinary criminal case direct evidence of the agreement alleged will very rarely be available; agreement is normally inferred from the subsequent acts of the defendants. If two gangs decide independently to rob the same bank on the same day and they are charged with conspiring together, they will find it difficult to satisfy the jury that they were not acting pursuant to some joint agreement.

Mere knowledge of or mental consent to a crime about to be com-

[52] 1962 Crim LR 458.
[53] 1876 2 QBD 48.

mitted by another does not make a man a conspirator, but quite a slight participation in the plan will be sufficient.

> 'A person may involve himself in the guilt of a conspiracy by his mere assent to and encouragement of the design, although nothing may have been assigned or intended to be executed by him personally' (Wright).[54]

But where something is assigned to an individual defendant, he must be aware of the broader plan[55]:

> 'any one of them may not know all the other parties; any one of them may not know the full extent of the scheme to which he attaches himself. What each must know, however, is that there is coming into existence, or is in existence, a scheme which goes beyond the illegal act which he agrees to do' (Paull J. in *R. v. Griffiths*).[56]

(b) *The Unlawful Act*

It has become commonplace in conspiracy cases to divide the unlawful acts necessary to establish liability into three categories: agreements to commit a crime, agreements to commit a tort or any other act giving rise to civil liability, and agreements to do a third class of acts which 'are not breaches of law at all, but which nevertheless are outrageously immoral or else, in some way, extremely injurious to the public.[57] A more detailed (and historically more correct) list of categories will be proposed below; but for the moment the orthodox classification will be followed.

I. *Agreements to commit a crime*

There can be no doubt that any agreement to commit a crime, however trivial, is punishable as a common law conspiracy. This was the Seventeenth Century Rule, and follows from the development of conspiracy by Star Chamber as an inchoate offence analogous to attempt. But unlike attempt (which is limited to indictable offences) a conspiracy to commit a purely *summary* offence is indictable: *Blamires Transport Services Ltd*,[58] approved by the House of Lords in *Kamara*.[59] It is immaterial that the crime which the defendant conspired to commit was in fact impossible: in *Whitchurch*[60] a girl who had not in fact been pregnant was convicted of conspiring to procure her own abortion.

[54] *Op cit* p. 70.
[55] This was one of the issues in *Prescott & Purdie:* see the reports in *The Times* November 10 – December 4 1971.
[56] 1965 2 All ER 448 at 453.
[57] See f. n. 43.
[58] 1964 1 QB 278.
[59] 1973 3 WLR 198.
[60] 1890 24 QBD 420.

II. *Agreements to commit a Tort or any other 'unlawful' act*

Until very recently it was thought that agreements to commit torts were indictable at common law only if they involved *fraud* or *malice*. Thus Smith & Hogan[61] say 'It is thought that it is certainly too wide to assert that a combination to commit any tort is a conspiracy. An agreement to commit a civil trespass is not indictable . . .' (p. 159), and in *Shaw v. D.P.P.*[62] Lord Reid said (at p. 456) 'it seems to be at least doubtful whether it is an offence to conspire to commit a tort which is neither malicious nor fraudulent nor accompanied by violence'.

But in the case of *Reg. v. Kamara*[63] the Court of Appeal in October 1972 threw all such limitations to the winds. The defendants were a group of students from Sierra Leone who as a protest against their government occupied its High Commission in London for a day in January 1971. They were charged with conspiring to trespass and with unlawful assembly and convicted on both counts. The most important question raised by their appeal was whether an agreement to commit any act of trespass constitutes a criminal conspiracy. After quoting the Denman formula from *Mulcahy*[64] ('a definition of conspiracy which has been given to juries by generations of judges and counsel') Lawton L.J. gave the answer of the Court in the following remarkable words:

> 'Whatever private views we may have about the desirability at the present time of having a definition of a crime in such wide terms, we feel bound to declare that the law is as stated by Willes J. in *Mulcahy*'s case, and if we apply the commonly held opinion that a tort is an unlawful act, it must follow that an agreement to trespass is an indictable conspiracy, no matter what absurd results can be envisaged if prosecutors and judges do not use common sense.
>
> We were urged by counsel for the Crown to set limits to this offence. He suggested two: first, that no agreement to trespass should be an indictable conspiracy unless there was an intent to injure and annoy; and secondly and alternatively that such an agreement should only be deemed criminal if its execution was likely to injure the public interest.
>
> We have been tempted to accept these submissions but we have reminded ourselves that we are judges, not legislators . . . we find and adjudge that there is an offence of conspiracy to trespass and that there are no such limitations upon it as counsel for the Crown suggested.'[65]

[61] *Criminal Law*, 2nd Edition (1969).
[62] 1961 2 All ER 446.
[63] 1972 3 All ER 999.
[64] LR 3 HL 306.
[65] 1972 3 All ER at 1004–1005.

It followed that for nine glorious months, until Kamara's case was heard by the House of Lords, a combination to commit *any* tort was a criminal offence. The consequences were, to say the least, wide-sweeping: if two people out for a walk in the country agreed to take a short cut across a field (an example given by Lawton L.J.), they were no longer merely civilly liable to the landowner (who would receive nominal damages and a heavy bill for costs if he brought legal proceedings), but they were now guilty of a criminal offence. The old sign Trespassers Will Be Prosecuted was not such a wooden lie after all!

But in July 1973 the House of Lords restored a modicum of sense to the law. Lord Hailsham, giving the main judgment of the House (with which Lord Morris of Borth-y-Gest and Lord Simon of Glaisdale concurred) made it clear that not all agreements to commit torts are indictable offences; but, he added, an agreement to commit a trespass *is* a crime if either

(1) the object of the agreement is the invasion of the public domain

or

(2) the defendants intend to inflict on the landowner something more than purely nominal damage.

> 'Trespass or any other form of tort can', he laid down, 'if intended, form the element of illegality necessary in conspiracy. But in my view more is needed. Either (1) Execution of the combination must invade the domain of the public, as, for instance, when the trespass involves the invasion of a building such as the Embassy of a friendly country or a publicly owned building, or (of course) where it infringes the criminal law ... Alternatively, (2) a combination to trespass becomes indictable if the execution of the combination necessarily involves and is known and intended to involve the infliction on its victim of something more than purely nominal damage. This must necessarily be the case where the intention is to occupy the premises to the exclusion of the owner's right, either by expelling him altogether (cf. *per* Lord Denman C.J. in *Kenrick* (1843) 5 QB 49 at 62) or otherwise effectively preventing him from enjoying his property.'[66]

Four points must be made about these two tests:

(1) They are intended to apply to *all* torts and not merely to trespass:

> '... a combination the execution of which has as its object not merely a tort or other actionable wrong, but also either the invasion of the public domain, or the intention to inflict on its victim injury and damage which goes beyond the field of the nominal is indictable, whether the object be achieved by trespass to land, goods or person,

[66] 1973 3 WLR 198 at 217.

by ruin of the reputation through the defamation of character, by the commission of private nuisance, by some contrivance of fraud, by the imposition of force, or by any other means which is tortious.'[67]

2) The first test, based on the 'invasion of the public domain', is identical to the limitation proposed by counsel for the prosecution, that agreements to commit a tort should only be criminal where they affect the public interest. At first sight it would appear that Lord Hailsham, by studiously eschewing the use of the words 'public interest', is trying to lay down a different test; but it is clear that the 'invasion of the public domain' is not limited to a purely physical dimension, *i.e.* the invasion of Embassies or publicly owned buildings, because:

a) Lord Hailsham intends the test to be applied to other torts, *e.g.* defamation, which do not involve the invasion of physical space

b) As his second example of invasion of the public domain Lord Hailsham cites trespasses which involve a breach of the criminal law, and for that reason enter the public domain

c) Lord Cross of Chelsea, the only other law Lord to deliver an opinion, does use the words 'public interest', and offers three criteria to identify those occasions when the public interest might be concerned:

> 'An agreement by several to commit acts which if done by one would only amount to a tort may constitute a criminal conspiracy if, as has been said, 'the public has a sufficient interest' – that is to say when the carrying into execution of the agreement would have consequences sufficiently harmful to call for penal sanctions. In the case of an agreement to trespass that might be the case – because, for example, of the nature of the property on which the trespass was to be committed or of the means to be employed in carrying out the trespass or of the object to be achieved by it.'[68]

3) The question whether the public interest is affected by an alleged conspiracy is a question of law for the judge and should not be left to the jury. Lord Hailsham disapproved the course adopted by Stable J. in *Bramley*,[69] who left to the jury the question whether a combination is sufficiently a matter of public concern to come within the ambit of the criminal law, and ruled instead that:

> 'The judge should direct the jury as to what element of fact if established to have been part of the agreement would be an invasion of the public field in either of the main ways I have described.'[70]

[67] *ibid.* at 216–7.
[68] *ibid.* at 219.
[69] (1946) 11 *Journal of Criminal Law* 36
[70] 1973 3 WLR at 217.

4) The effect of Lord Hailsham's second test, making criminal any combination to commit a tort which involves an intention to inflict on the victim more than purely nominal damage, is much harder to assess. It is clearly not the same as the second test proposed by the Crown, that an agreement to commit a tort should become indictable when its execution includes an element of fraud, or the use of force, or an intent to injure or annoy; because the emphasis in that test is on the means employed by the conspirators, whereas Lord Hailsham's test is based on their intention.

Rather, Lord Hailsham's test would appear to be closer to the old test of 'malice', in the sense given to it by the authors of a recent article in the Criminal Law Review, 'Conspiring to Squat'.[71] The article argues that a distinction should be drawn between a mere act of trespass to property, where the defendants' intention is simply to commit the act and not the trespass, and an intended trespass meant to infringe another's rights. The latter case should be indictable as a conspiracy, the former not. This distinction they illustrated by reference to two cases cited in *Kamara*, *Turner* (1811)[72] and *Levy* (1819).[73] In *Turner* a number of men trespassed on the prosecutor's land at night, armed with cudgels, with intent to poach hares; they were prosecuted for conspiracy, but found not guilty, Lord Ellenborough C.J. observing (at p. 358)

> 'But I should be sorry that the cases in conspiracy against individuals, which have gone far enough, should be pushed still further: I should be sorry to have it doubted whether persons agreeing to go and sport upon another's ground, in other words, to commit a civil trespass, should be thereby in peril of an indictment for an offence which would subject them to infamous punishment.'

This decision was almost certainly wrong; Lord Campbell C.J. pointed out in *Rowlands* (1851) 17 QB 671 that the trespassers, being armed to overcome any opposition, were guilty of unlawful assembly and so should have been found guilty of conspiracy to commit a crime. But the principle laid down by Lord Ellenborough has been approved in subsequent cases – *e.g. Seward* (1834) and *Kenrick* (1843) – and in *Kamara* the House of Lords recognised, which the Court of Appeal had signally failed to do, that *Rowlands* had not overruled *Turner*; and both Lord Hailsham and Lord Cross of Chelsea approved Lord Ellenborough's sentiments.

By contrast in *Levy* the defendants were found guilty of conspiracy in that they had conspired together to injure and terrify a woman,

[71] 1971 Crim. L.R. 342 (Davies, Dashwood and Trice).
[72] 13 East 228; 104 ER 357.
[73] 2 Stark 458; 171 ER 704.

when she was giving birth to a child, by making loud noises and by knocking violently against the wall of the house in which she lay. The authors conclude:

> 'The gravamen of the offence it would now appear is the motive, common design or purpose of the conspirators (*i.e.* the intention to infringe the right and not the intention to commit the act which causes the wrong) and nothing more. The result of this analysis is that both *Turner* and *Levy* can be reconciled: in *Turner,* the intention of the men was merely to follow game on another person's land (and not to violate his rights); whereas in *Levy,* the intention of the conspirators was to injure or interfere with the pregnant woman's rights.'[74]

In the event in *Kamara* the convictions were upheld only on the narrow ground of the first test, that the public interest was involved, because the indictment did not recite any particulars of the defendants' intentions: 'count one of the indictment was not drawn so as to include specific reference to the elements recited above except . . . the invasion of the High Commission. The conviction on the first count can, therefore, only be sustained on the last and narrow ground'.[75]

Evidence of harm to the public interest in *Kamara* is not hard to find: 'in this case the public interest was clearly involved', Lawton L.J. had suggested in the Court of Appeal, 'first because of the special position of the High Commission premises under the Diplomatic Privileges Act, 1964, and secondly because conduct of the kind proved at the trial was likely to cause a breach of the peace'.[76] Although difficult to define, this requirement of harm to the *public* has a long and respectable pedigree in the law of conspiracy: for example in the *Mogul Steamship*[77] case Lord Bramwell qualified many of the more sweeping *dicta* based on Hawkins[78] by saying (at p. 48):

> 'Where the violation of a private right is an actionable wrong, a combination to violate it, *if the public has a sufficient interest,* is a crime' (italics added).

If certain combinations to commit torts are to be criminal (and it will be argued in chapter 9 that *none* should be) this seems a sensible limitation of criminality: for criminal sanctions should really be invoked in cases of injury to the public, and not merely where some private right is infringed.

[74] 1971 Crim. L.R. at 351.
[75] *per* Lord Hailsham, 1973 3 WLR at 217.
[76] 1972 3 All ER at 1005.
[77] 1892 AC 25.
[78] See p. 16.

Whether there are any other classes of unlawful act under head (ii) which become criminal in combination (for example a conspiracy to procure a breach of contract) will be discussed in the more detailed classification of the authorities below. But it is possible that as a result of the decision in *Hain* (1972)[78a] a conspiracy to harm a person in a way which is not even tortious may yet give rise to criminal liability. Peter Hain was the organizer of a number of campaigns to prevent South African sporting teams from coming to England, and to hinder and disrupt the activities of those teams which came. His activities were brought to the attention of the Director of Public Prosecutions, who declined to prosecute; but a private prosecution was then mounted by a barrister named Francis Bennion.

Unfortunately for Bennion the Court of Appeal reserved its judgment in *Kamara* until after his prosecution had been launched; so that the indictment in *Hain* was not founded on conspiracy to trespass (a charge to which after *Kamara* Hain would have had little defence). The indictment was based instead on the fact that he had conspired to 'hinder disrupt interfere with and prevent the exercise of the lawful rights of persons to play or watch and otherwise peaceably to enjoy' the rugby game/cricket match *etc*. On one of the counts worded in this way, involving the disruption of the Davis Cup tennis match in Bristol, Hain was convicted. The full significance of his case cannot be assessed until it is commented on by the Court of Appeal in the light of the House of Lords' decision in *Kamara*; but insofar as a combination may prevent people from exercising their 'lawful rights' without actually committing a tort, and still be guilty of criminal conspiracy, *Hain* goes beyond *Kamara*. But for the moment *Kamara* being a decision of the House of Lords is much the more important case.

III. *The third head – conspiracy to commit a public mischief etc.*

It is now beyond all doubt that the offences of conspiracy to effect a public mischief, conspiracy to corrupt public morals and conspiracy to outrage public decency are all crimes recognized by English law. Whether the latter two types of conspiracy were created by the House of Lords or whether they had previously existed at common law, and whether they are sub-categories of conspiracy to effect a public mischief or separate categories of their own is unimportant for our present purpose: the fact is that they now *exist*. In 1961 in the case of *Shaw v D.P.P.*[79] the House of Lords held by 4:1 that the offence of conspiracy to corrupt public morals existed at common law; and in 1972 in the prosecution of IT, *Reg. v. Knuller,*[80] the House of Lords reaffirmed *Shaw,* two law Lords[81] holding that it had been rightly

[78a] *Times* 28 July–22 August 1972.
[79] 1961 2 All ER 446.
[80] 1972 3 WLR 143.
[81] Lord Morris of Borth-y-Gest and Lord Kilbrandon

decided, and three[82] holding that even if *Shaw* was wrongly decided it must stand until altered by Parliament. Furthermore in *Knuller* the House of Lords held (Lord Reid and Lord Diplock dissenting) that a conspiracy to outrage public decency is an offence known to the common law. As for conspiracy to effect a public mischief, in *Newland*[83] Lord Goddard C.J. said (at p. 165),

> 'It is much too late to object that a conspiracy to effect a public mischief is an offence unknown to the law. There have been at least three reported cases during the present century in which that charge has been made and convictions upheld.'

This statement was quoted approvingly by Lord Tucker in *Shaw*, and in *D.P.P. v. Bhagwan*[84] (1970) the question was not even argued; Lord Diplock, giving the judgment of the House of Lords, spoke of 'the established categories of public mischief'.[85]

There can no longer be any doubt that these three types of conspiracy are now part of our law; but what kind of conduct they make criminal is still by no means certain. To this question we now turn.

Conspiracy to corrupt public morals

The leading case on conspiracy to corrupt public morals is still *Shaw v. D.P.P.* Shaw was charged as a result of publishing a magazine called the *Ladies Directory*, which contained the names, addresses and telephone numbers of prostitutes, with occasional nude photographs and details of specialities or perversions. The indictment against him charged him with three offences: (1) conspiring to corrupt public morals, (2) living on the earnings of prostitution and (3) publishing an obscene publication. Counts (2) and (3) were statutory offences;[86] the conspiracy count was included by the prosecution because there was some doubt as to whether his conduct amounted to 'living on' immoral earnings, and whether his publication could tend to deprave and corrupt if the men who bought the *Ladies Directory* were corrupted already. He was in fact convicted on all three counts: and he appealed to the House of Lords against his conviction on counts (1) and (2). The House upheld his conviction on both counts.

The first question raised by *Shaw*, which is still not decided, is whether he was guilty on count (1) because the corruption of public morals is itself an indictable offence (in which case he was guilty of a conspiracy to commit a *crime*, and the third head is unnecessary), or

[82] Lord Reid, Lord Morris and Lord Simon of Glaisdale. Lord Morris said 'There comes a time when further disputation should cease' (p. 155)
[83] 1954 1 QB 158.
[84] 1970 3 All ER 97.
[85] 1970 3 All ER at 105.
[86] Sexual Offences Act 1956, s.30; Obscene Publications Act 1959, s.2.

whether it was the element of *conspiracy* which made his conduct unlawful. The Court of Criminal Appeal held that such conduct was criminal whether done by a group or by an individual:

> 'It is an established principle of common law', Ashworth J. said, 'that conduct calculated or intended to corrupt public morals (as opposed to the morals of a particular individual) is an indictable misdemeanour.'[87]

In the House of Lords the question was not expressly decided. Lord Tucker said:

> 'the decision of this case does not depend on a detailed examination of the old authorities in order to ascertain whether, in every case, the act or acts in question, whether performed or proposed, constituted common law misdemeanours in themselves at the date of the decisions';[88]

it was not necessary to decide this question because

> 'it has for long been accepted that there are some conspiracies which are criminal although the acts agreed to be done are not *per se* criminal or tortious if done by individuals'.[89]

Nevertheless he did not dissociate himself from the opinions expressed in the Court of Criminal Appeal; while Viscount Simonds and Lord Morris were fairly clearly in agreement with the Court of Criminal Appeal, and Lord Hodson probably so.[90]

The next reported case on conspiracy to corrupt public morals is *Knuller*.[91] The defendants were directors of the underground newspaper IT, which carried in its personal column advertisements from homosexuals. They were charged with conspiracy to corrupt public morals and conspiracy to outrage public decency and convicted on both counts.

The speeches in *Knuller* throw no further light on the question whether the corruption of public morals is in itself criminal; they merely re-affirm the decision in *Shaw,* that a *conspiracy* to corrupt public morals is an indictable offence, without asking (except for Lord Diplock, who dissented) why or how. In any case the question, although very important in principle,[92] is perhaps not so important in

[87] 1962 AC 220 at 233.
[88] 1961 2 All ER 446 at 463.
[89] *Ibid* at p. 461.
[90] He expressed agreement with the speeches of both Viscount Simonds and Lord Tucker.
[91] *Supra.*
[92] Because it reflects on the authority of cases like *Manley* 1933 1 KB 529.

practice, because in the cases on corrupting public morals it is very unusual to find one defendant acting entirely on his own: out of the 33 successful prosecutions for conspiracy to corrupt public morals from *Shaw* (prosecuted in 1959) to *Knuller* (prosecuted in 1969) there were only two cases (*Shaw* itself and *Saltzer* in 1966) in which only one defendant was convicted,[93] and so long as there is *some* evidence of other parties to a conspiracy the defendant can always be charged with conspiring 'with others unknown'.[93a]

It remains to describe what sort of conduct is considered by the courts to be corrupting of public morals. Here *Knuller* has added something to our understanding of what is meant by 'corruption'. The House of Lords in *Shaw* approved a direction to the jury in which the trial judge said 'I wonder really whether it means in this case and in this context much more than lead astray morally';[94] and of this direction Lord Reid said in *Knuller*:[95]

> 'I cannot agree that that is right. "Corrupt" is a strong word and the jury ought to be reminded of that, as they were in the present case. The Obscene Publications Act appears to use the words "deprave" and "corrupt" as synonymous, as I think they are. We may regret that we live in a permissive society but I doubt whether even the most staunch defender of a better age would maintain that all or even most of those who have at one time or in one way or another been led astray morally have thereby become depraved or corrupted. I think that the jury should be told in one way or another that although in the end the question whether matter is corrupting is for them, they should keep in mind the current standards of ordinary decent people.'

This last sentence, and in particular the yardstick of 'the current standards of ordinary decent people' reveals just how vague the legal definition of corruption still (inevitably) is. Lord Simon of Glaisdale agreed that 'lead astray morally' is too broad a test; but his proposed alternative, that 'the words "corrupt public morals" suggest conduct which a jury might find to be destructive of the very fabric of society',[96] is even more uncertain.

Lord Reid also had something to say on what is meant by '*public*' morals:

> 'Conspiracy to corrupt public morals is something of a misnomer.

[93] Answer given by the Attorney-General to a question in Hansard, 30 June 1972 Col 427.
[93a] *Sed quaere:* see *Oswin* 1964 Crim LR 479, discussed *infra* on p. 120.
[94] See 1962 AC at 290
[95] 1972 3 WLR at 148.
[96] 1972 3 WLR at 180. The test is presumably derived from Devlin: *The Enforcement of Morals*. For a critique of Lord Devlin's 'disintegration thesis', and an interesting comparison between Devlin and Durkheim, see Hart 1967 U. Chi. L.R. 1.

It really means to corrupt the morals of such members of the public as may be influenced by the matter published by the accused.'[97]

And it is apparent from the other speeches that anybody who comes into contact with a publication may be influenced by it – the appeal of the advertisements in the 'MALES' section of IT was not confined to homosexuals. Thus Lord Morris of Borth-y-Gest said:

'In criticism of the summing up of the learned judge it was submitted that the jury should have been told that if they considered that the advertisements were only addressed to those who already indulged in homosexual conduct then they (the jury) should acquit. The criticism is ill-founded. In the first place, a casual perusal of the advertisements reveals that it could not rationally be held that they were only so addressed or directed: in the second place, it is a fallacy to assume . . . that someone cannot be corrupted more than once.'

Examples of the advertisements attacked in IT are:

'Young gay male desperately needs to earn £40 as soon as possible. Will do anything legal. Genuine replies only please.'

'Young dolly boy seeks sugar daddy. Photo appreciated.'[98]

'Pretty dolly boy wanted for sex and travel by boy, 21. Ample bread.'

'Ex French Foreign legionnaire, handsome, active 25, seeks assistance from gentleman of means. Anything legal considered.'[99]

Of the first of these advertisements Lord Simon of Glaisdale remarked:

'In its context this could hardly be read as other than an offer of sexual prostitution; it differs from the advertisements in 'The Ladies Directory' only in that it was apparently made by a male rather than a female.'[100]

This was the conduct which was held to be corrupting of public morals in *Knuller*. The particulars of the offence charged in the indictment were that Knuller Ltd. and the three directors of IT 'conspired together and with persons inserting advertisements in issues of a magazine entitled "IT" under the heading "MALES", and with other persons unknown by means of the said magazine and the said advertisements to induce readers thereof to meet those persons inserting such advertisements for the purpose of sexual practices taking place

[97] 1972 3 WLR at 148.
[98] Quoted by Lord Simon of Glaisdale, *ibid.* at 172–3.
[99] Quoted by Lord Hailsham in the House of Lords debate on the Criminal Justice Bill, Hansard 27 July 1972 col 1568.
[100] 1972 3 WLR at 173.

between male persons and to encourage readers thereof to indulge in such practices, with intent thereby to debauch and corrupt the morals as well of youth as of divers other liege subjects of Our Lady the Queen'.

In *Shaw* the indictment was worded in similar language, but the *Ladies Directory* was a rather different class of publication from IT, since the only (and overt) purpose of the whole magazine was to attract custom for prostitutes, driven off the streets by the Street Offences Act 1957. Shaw should nevertheless be spared some sympathy since according to an article in the Harvard Law Review[101] he had been assured by counsel that the venture would be legal, and he had also left a copy of the first issue with Scotland Yard.

Shaw and *Knuller* are the only reported cases of prosecutions brought since 1959 for conspiracy to corrupt public morals. But the Attorney-General told the House of Commons in June 1972 that there had been 31 other successful prosecutions;[102] and some information about these other cases was given by the Lord Chancellor in the House of Lords debate on the Criminal Justice Bill on 27 July 1972. He told the House:

> 'I do not know what they were all for. I think there were about 30 between the *Ladies Directory* and *Knuller*. But most of them were for "blue" films ... the "blue" films are straight questions of obscenity – people who allow themselves to be photographed copulating in various positions and displays for the purpose of commercial exploitation.'[103]

The reason for using the conspiracy charge in most of these cases is that because of a loophole in the Obscene Publications Act a blue film can be prosecuted for obscenity only if it is shown in a private house; if it is shown in a factory or a club no statutory offence is committed.

These then are the sort of cases which have been held to constitute conspiracies to corrupt public morals – publishing advertisements from prostitutes, male and female; showing 'blue' films; publishing advertisements from married people seeking other sexual partners is a hypothetical example given by Lord Morris of Borth-y-Gest;[104] 'a conspiracy to encourage and promote lesbianism today, or incestuous sexual intercourse in the year 1907' (before incest was made a criminal offence) are two more suggestions from Lord Tucker;[105] and in the trial of *Last Exit to Brooklyn*[106] the Court of Appeal, interpreting 'corrupt' in s.1 of the Obscene Publications Act 1959, said:

[101] 75 Harv. LR 1652.
[102] See note 93 *supra*.
[103] Hansard 27 July 1972 col 1569.
[104] In *Knuller* 1972 2 All ER at 907.
[105] In *Shaw* 1961 2 All ER at 463.
[106] *R v. Calder & Boyars Ltd.* 1969 1 QB 151.

'The corruption may also take various forms. It may be to induce erotic desires of a heterosexual kind, or to promote homosexuality or other sexual perversions or drug taking or brutal violence.'

This suggestion that corruption might extend to activities outside the sexual field was eventually followed in a conspiracy case early in 1973, *Reg. v. Brooks and others*[107] when Miss Brooks and 20 others were charged with 43 separate offences under the Dangerous Drugs Act relating to their possession of Chinese heroin. But, lurking at the very end of their indictment, count 44 read:

'Conspiracy to Corrupt Public Morals.
Particulars of Offence: Gloria Anne Brooks [and others] on divers days between the 1st day of January and the 26th day of February, 1972, conspired together and with other persons unknown to corrupt the morals of such persons as might consume heroin by procuring quantities of heroin and supplying the same to members of the public in and in the vicinity of Gerrard Street, London W.1.'

Presumably (there seems no other explanation) the count was included in case the defendants were acquitted on the substantive charges.

The field is thus very wide – and growing wider. Which activities from this list are prosecuted as conspiracies to corrupt public morals depends entirely on the discretion of the prosecuting authorities;[108] and whether those prosecutions result in convictions depends on the jury's interpretation of what are 'the current standards of ordinary decent people', or what tends to be 'destructive of the very fabric of society'.[109]

Conspiracy to outrage public decency

Here again it is uncertain whether there is a substantive offence at common law of conduct which outrages public decency. Lord Reid and Lord Diplock argued in *Knuller* that there is no such general offence, but only a number of particular offences involving indecency (such as indecent exposure). Lord Morris of Borth-y-Gest and Lord Simon of Glaisdale both held that there was such an offence, and cited as their authority none other than Lord Reid in *Shaw,* where he had said:

'I think that they [*i.e.* the authorities] establish that it is an indictable offence to say or do or exhibit anything in public which

[107] *New Statesman* 23 February 1973 p. 265.

[108] For an interesting attempt by a private citizen to force the police to increase their activities against the sellers of pornographic literature, see *Reg v Metropolitan Police Commissioner, ex parte Blackburn,* Times Law Report, October 30 and November 27 1972. Blackburn's application was dismissed, but his efforts evoked considerable judicial sympathy.

[109] Tests proposed by Lord Reid and Lord Simon of Glaisdale respectively. See footnotes 95 and 96.

outrages public decency, whether or not it also tends to corrupt and deprave those who see or hear it.'[110]

Lord Kilbrandon, holding the balance, said rather cautiously,

> 'the relevance of a charge of outraging public decency by a public invitation to indulge in sexual perversion appears to be supported by all the speeches in *Shaw v. D.P.P.*';[110a]

but it is not clear whether he is referring to the charge in the indictment, which was a conspiracy charge, or a charge of the substantive offence. *Mayling*[111] is authority of the Court of Criminal Appeal that there is a general offence of committing an act outraging public decency.

But once again this question is not directly relevant to a study of conspiracy, because the House of Lords clearly held in *Knuller* that a *conspiracy* to outrage public decency is an offence known to the law. Of what does the offence consist? The only law Lord who dealt with this question in any detail was Lord Simon of Glaisdale:

> 'I turn, then, to the requirement of publicity. *Reg. v. Mayling* (1963) 2 QB 717 shows that the substantive offence (and therefore the conduct the subject of the conspiracy) must be committed in public, in the sense that the circumstances must be such that the alleged outrageously indecent matter could have been seen by more than one person, even though in fact no more than one did see it. If it is capable of being seen by one person only no offence is committed ...
>
> It was argued for the Crown that it was immaterial whether or not the alleged outrage to decency took place in public, provided that the sense of decency of the public or a substantial section of the public was outraged. But this seems to me to be contrary to many of the authorities ... "public" refers to the place in which the offence is committed. This is borne out by the way the rule was framed by my noble and learned friend, Lord Reid, in *Shaw v. D.P.P.*.. It is also borne out by what is presumably the purpose of the legal rule – namely, that reasonable people may venture out in public without the risk of outrage to certain minimum accepted standards of decency.
>
> On the other hand, I do not think that it would necessarily negative the offence that the act or exhibit is superficially hid from view, if the public is expressly or impliedly invited to penetrate the cover.

[110] 1962 AC at 281.
[110a] 1972 3 WLR 143 at 186–7.
[111] 1963 2 QB 717.

Thus, the public touting for an outrageously indecent exhibition in private would not escape: see *Reg. v. Saunders,* 1 Q.B.D. 15. Another obvious example is an outrageously indecent exhibit with a cover entitled "Lift in order to see . . ."

There are other features of the offence which should, in my view, be brought to the notice of the jury. It should be emphasised that "outrage" like "corrupt", is a very strong word. "Outraging public decency" goes considerably beyond offending the susceptibilities of, or even shocking, reasonable people. Moreover, the offence is, in my view, concerned with recognised minimum standards of decency, which are likely to vary from time to time. Finally, notwithstanding that "public" in the offence is used in a location sense, public decency must be viewed as a whole; and I think the jury should be invited, where appropriate, to remember that they live in a plural society, with a tradition of tolerance towards minorities, and that this atmosphere of toleration is itself part of public decency.'[112]

This was the only speech which dealt at any length with the new offence of conspiracy to outrage public decency. As some indication of the stringency of the test proposed by Lord Simon, the convictions of the defendants on the public decency count were quashed by the House of Lords; but that is not quite the same as an acquittal – it is impossible to say whether, if the judge's summing-up had been correct, the defendants in *Knuller* would have been acquitted or convicted. What can be said with some emphasis is that however stringent the test of 'outrage' and of 'public', the offence must always set a lesser standard than conspiracy to corrupt public morals. 'Outrage', like 'corrupt' may be a very strong word; but it can never be *as* strong as corrupt. The two offences are in a sense complementary, since those upright citizens who are not corrupted may well be outraged; and those who are not outraged by certain displays must presumably already be corrupted (which does not prevent them from being further corrupted, or even from being 're-corrupted', according to the House of Lords in *D.P.P. v. Whyte*).[113]

Conspiracy to effect a public mischief

Yet again, it is uncertain whether causing a public mischief is an indictable offence in the individual. In *Manley*[114] the Court of Criminal Appeal upheld the conviction for effecting a public mischief of a woman who had wasted the time of the police by giving false information that she had been assaulted and robbed. The principle of that decision, that courts may declare acts to be criminal which they con-

[112] 1972 3 WLR at 183–4.
[113] 1972 3 All ER 12.
[114] 1933 1 KB 529.

sider to be contrary to public policy, was heavily criticised at the time;[115] and in *Newland*,[116] Lord Goddard C.J. (at p. 168) said:

> 'with all respect to a case which, as we have said, is binding on us we believe that the right approach to what may be compendiously called public mischief cases is to regard them as part of the law of conspiracy, and to hold the actions of an individual not committed in combination with others as indictable only if they constitute what has been held in the past to be common law or statutory offences'.

After *Newland* it was thought by many people that *Manley* was a dead letter.[117] But then in *Shaw v. D.P.P.* (which was just as much a public mischief case as one on public morals)[118] Viscount Simonds delivered the following trenchant statement:

> 'When Lord Mansfield speaking long after the Star Chamber had been abolished said that the Court of King's Bench was the *custos morum* of the people and had superintendency of offences *contra bones mores,* he was asserting, as I now assert, that there is in that Court a residual power, where no statute has yet intervened to supersede the common law, to superintend those offences which are prejudicial to the public welfare. Such occasions will be rare, for Parliament has not been slow to legislate when attention has been sufficiently aroused. But gaps remain and will always remain, since no one can foresee every way in which the wickedness of man may disrupt the order of society.'[119]

Once again there was a storm of criticism,[120] and once again a policy of judicial retreat. All the law Lords in *Knuller* (except for Lord Diplock) went out of their way to say that the decision in *Shaw* was not to be taken as lending any support to the doctrine that the courts have some general or residual power either to create new offences, or to widen existing offences so that conduct of a type not previously criminal becomes punishable – which represents a complete denial of Viscount Simonds' assertion. In between these judicial advances and retreats, it is difficult to say what exactly the status of *Manley* now is; it was not referred to by the House of Lords in *Shaw* or *Bhagwan*,[121] and was mentioned in *Knuller* only by Lord Diplock. Probably in view

[115] See Stallybrass in 49 LQR 183.
[116] 1954 1 QB 158.
[117] The question is briefly discussed in the Criminal Law Revision Committee's Seventh Report, on Felonies and Misdemeanours, Cmnd 2659.
[118] See for example Viscount Simonds at 1961 2 All ER 452, Lord Tucker at 463.
[119] 1961 2 All ER at 452.
[120] Of the flood of literature on *Shaw* see especially Brownlie & Williams *Judicial Legislation in Criminal Law* 1964 Can. Bar R. 561; and for the wider issue of the legal enforcement of morality, see Hart: *Law, Liberty & Morality* (1963).
[121] 1970 3 All ER 97.

of the categorical denials of the Simonds doctrine in *Knuller* and the whole tenor of the judgment in *Bhagwan, Manley* is now a dead letter; but the judicial pendulum may swing again and even now not all the law Lords have renounced the Simonds doctrine. Speaking in a House of Lords debate in 1972, Lord Hailsham said that one of the questions raised by *Shaw* was

> 'had the courts still got . . . a residual right to extend the Common Law in the field of substantive offences? I think *Shaw* decides that they have. . . . It may or may not be true that this is overstepping the bounds of what the Judiciary is about. I personally like a bit of Common Law which is furry at the edges and which has a few growing points.'[122]

As for the offence of *conspiracy* to cause a public mischief (as opposed to causing a public mischief *simpliciter*, the charge in *Manley*), it is hard to see that its scope is significantly diminished by the recent judicial retreat. The retreat is basically a retreat from *obiter dicta*,[123] a disclaimer of some of the more embarrassing things that Viscount Simonds said, rather than a real change in policy: in *Knuller*, after all, *Shaw* and its *ratio decidendi* (as laid down by Lord Tucker) were re-affirmed. A good example of the Lords' main concern is provided by this heroic re-interpretation of the Simonds doctrine:

> 'it seems at least probable that in these *dicta* the noble Lord was intending to give an account of how the crime of conspiracy to corrupt public morals first came to be recognised . . .'[124]

Nowhere in *Knuller* or in *Bhagwan*[125] is there an express disclaimer of the courts' powers to classify new fact-situations as *conspiracies to effect a public mischief*; and indeed in a field which contains a case-law so varied as the public mischief cases, the offence of conspiracy to effect a public michief is meaningless unless it *can* be applied to new fact-situations.

Bhagwan, however, was hailed by some commentators as laying down a ruling that the categories of public mischief are now closed;[126] but any doubt on this matter has now been laid to rest by the House of Lords' decision in *Kamara.*[127] Lord Hailsham, giving the judgment of the House, declared:

> 'I do not regard the categories of conspiracy to effect a public mischief as closed, or even as capable of being closed, but extension

[122] Hansard 27 July 1972 col. 1566.
[123] See Lord Kilbrandon in *Knuller* 1972 3 WLR at 185G.
[124] *ibid.* at 186.
[125] 1970 3 All ER 97.
[126] See, *e.g.*, the case-note in 34 M.L.R. 81.
[127] 1973 3 WLR 198.

should be very closely and jealously watched by the Courts, owing to the difficulty of riding the horse of public policy and the danger of applying the subjective criteria of individual judges to the concept.'[128]

Conspiracy to effect a public mischief is not therefore a fossil category, as some had supposed, but on the contrary is very much alive (see the list of unreported cases at the end of this section)[128a] and is capable of further extension, subject to the constraints noted by Lord Hailsham above.

It remains to consider what is meant by 'public mischief'. The field is enormously wide; Smith & Hogan[129] say rather despairingly,

> 'How far it extends is undetermined for the courts have as yet laid down no guiding principles beyond the fact that the object of the parties must be mischievous to the public.'

But in truth this is because the public mischief category has been used as a sort of catch-all device into which a lot of conspiracy cases have been swept which properly belong in class (i) – agreements to commit a crime – or which are better subsumed under the old-established heads of conspiracy to defraud, conspiracy to cheat a government department, conspiracy to pervert the course of justice, *etc.* In the more detailed classification set out at the end of this section the public mischief cases will be re-arranged under these separate heads; but for the moment it is convenient to discuss them all under this general heading.

The first of the reported cases is Higgins (1801).[130] The only connection this case has with public mischief is the sweeping *obiter dictum* given by Lawrence J. that

> 'all offences of a public nature, that is, all such acts or attempts as tend to the prejudice of the public, are indictable';

but no other member of the court stated the law in such wide terms, and the statement was quite unnecessary to the court's decision, which turned on the law of incitement and attempt. The Court of Criminal Appeal applied the dictum in *Manley* (1933).[131]

The next case is *de Berenger*,[132] which involved an agreement to raise the price of government stocks by circulating false rumours of the death of Napoleon. Three of the judges in this case appeared to base

[128] *ibid.* at 210.
[128a] At pp. 43–44.
[129] *Op. cit.* 2nd Edn p. 160.
[130] 1801 2 East 5.
[131] 1933 1 KB 529, *supra.*
[132] 1814 3 M & S 67.

their decision on a conspiracy to defraud; only Lord Ellenborough C.J. mentioned public mischief, and according to Wright[133] that was quite unnecessary because the circulation of false news in order to disturb markets or prices was an indictable offence anyway. *De Berenger* was therefore either a conspiracy to defraud or an agreement to commit a crime.

Similar cases to *de Berenger* were *Lewis* (1869)[134] and *Aspinall* (1876).[135] *Lewis* involved a conspiracy to defraud the public by means of a mock auction in which the bidders were not genuine and bid only to force up the prices. *Aspinall* was a conspiracy to cheat and defraud prospective purchasers of shares by a false prospectus.

Also in the middle of the nineteenth century are two public morals cases which have occasionally been classified as conspiracies to effect a public mischief:[136] *Howell* (1864)[137] which was a conspiracy to procure a woman to become a prostitute, and *Mears* (1851),[138] a conspiracy to defile a girl of fifteen (not at that time a crime). It will be argued in the revised classification presented below that the public morals cases should properly be considered as a separate category.

Brailsford (1905),[139] the next reported case, charged the two defendants with unlawfully conspiring to obtain a passport in the name of one of them for a third party, 'by false representations and in fraud of the Foreign Office regulations, to the public mischief and to the endangerment of peaceful relations between the King and the Czar'. The indictment in fact contained a second count, of obtaining a passport by false pretences, and Lord Alverstone C.J. said

> 'It is not necessary for us to decide whether apart from conspiracy the obtaining of a passport by false pretences ... is of itself a misdemeanour',

but the opinion of the court is fairly clear that it was. Furthermore since *Board of Trade v. Owen*[140] such behaviour amounts to a conspiracy to defraud: Lord Tucker said that the matters alleged in *Owen* were correctly described as conspiracy to defraud, since a Government department acts to its detriment if it issues a licence which enables something to be done which the department is charged with a duty to prevent.

In *Porter* (1910)[141] the two defendants entered into £50 recognisances for the appearance in court of a third man, and at the same

[133] *op. cit.* p. 29
[134] 11 Cox 404.
[135] 1 QBD 730; 2 QBD 48.
[136] *E.g.* by Lord Tucker in *Shaw* 1961 2 All ER at 464 and by Lord Hailsham in *Kamara*, 1973 3 WLR at 210.
[137] 4 F & F 160.
[138] 2 Den. 79.
[139] 1905 2 KB 730.
[140] 1957 AC 602.
[141] 1910 1 KB 369.

time agreed with that man that he should indemnify them against their liability. The Court of Criminal Appeal said:

> 'Jelf J. rightly held that the agreement entered into by the appellant was an illegal contract, . . . as being one which clearly tended to produce a public mischief, and that it amounted to a criminal conspiracy, without any necessity for a finding by the jury that there was an intent to pervert or obstruct the course of justice.'

Here again such a wide *ratio decidendi* was not necessary to the decision: the agreement to indemnify bail may be regarded as a species of contempt of court, and the conviction for conspiracy could have rested on that foundation.

In *Meyrick* (1929)[142] the two defendants were night club owners who bribed a police officer not to enforce the licensing laws. Although convicted of conspiracy to effect a public mischief, they were also found guilty of conspiracy to pervert the course of justice. The first count of the indictment charged them and the police sergeant with 'conspiracy to contravene the provisions of the licensing Acts by the unlawful sale of intoxicating liquors and to effect a public mischief by obstructing the police of the Metropolis in the execution of their public duty and by corrupting officers of that force . . . and thereby to prevent the due administration of the law and prevent (*sic*) the course of public justice'.[143] Such a count appears to be bad for duplicity, since it charges at least two separate offences in the one count; and furthermore it appears at least in part to contain a 'roll-up' charge,[144] since each of the defendants was also convicted of a substantive offence under the Prevention of Corruption Act 1906.

In *Bassey* (1931)[145] the defendant gained admission to the Inner Temple by submitting forged certificates. As well as being convicted for conspiracy to commit a public mischief, he was found guilty of forgery and uttering forged documents. Of this case Lord Hailsham said in the House of Lords debate referred to above:[146]

> 'In the case of *Bassey* there was a conspiracy to obtain admission to the Bar by obtaining false certificates. Again, obviously it was a criminal conspiracy. What makes it illegal at the moment is the law of conspiracy, and if the Amendment of the noble Baroness [Birk] were passed it would cease to be a crime.'[147]

[142] 21 Cr App R 94.
[143] 21 Cr App R 94. Presumably 'prevent' in the report should read 'pervert'.
[144] For which see below, p. 73.
[145] 22 Cr App R 160.
[146] See footnote 122
[147] Hansard 24 July 1972 cols 1126, 7. Lady Birk's amendment limited conspiracy to agreements to commit crimes. Lord Hailsham's treatment of the other public mischief cases was similarly misleading.

This is simply untrue, as a reading of almost any of the basic textbooks would show:[148] the convictions for forgery and uttering forged documents were quite sufficient.

Leese,[149] a case in the 1930s involving the publication of articles in *The Fascist* newspaper attacking the Jews, was a case where the defendants were convicted of creating a public mischief, but surprisingly they were acquitted of sedition. This is strange because Stephen's common law definition of sedition, adopted in *Burns*,[150] includes as one of its elements the promotion of 'feelings of illwill and hostility between different classes of Her Majesty's subjects'. Nowadays the conspiracy charge in such a case would be unnecessary because such conduct would probably be caught by the Race Relations Act.[151]

In *Young*[152] (1944) the defendant, a clerk of the works to Hammersmith Borough Council, conspired with a building contractor to erect air raid shelters which fell far short of the Home Office specifications. The indictment contained seven counts, and included a charge of obtaining by false pretences the sums paid to the building contractor and conspiring to commit a public mischief. The defendant was acquitted on the false pretences charge but convicted of conspiracy. On the face of it this appears to be a case where the public mischief charge was necessary to obtain a conviction; but (a) the report does not reveal what the other counts were in the indictment (apart from a charge of manslaughter, which was withdrawn) (b) the facts would seem to support a charge of conspiracy to defraud.

Newland (1954)[153] is another case where at first sight the public mischief change appears to be the only one available. It involved an agreement to divert decorated pottery from the export to the home market, a manoeuvre which did not directly contravene the relevant Statutory Orders but was in flagrant defiance of the government's declared policy. However an examination of the case reveals that the defendants were probably guilty of forgery and of fraud, and that conspiracy to commit a public mischief was a 'roll-up' charge heading an indictment of 13 counts. On the conspiracy charge the particulars of the offence were 'that the appellants ... conspired together ... by fraudulent means to obtain, and by dishonest devices to distribute ...'; and Lord Goddard C.J. implied in his judgement (on p. 166) that the defendants had obtained the pottery by making false representations and using fraudulent documents.

The next public mischief case is *Shaw v. D.P.P.* (1961) which has

[148] See, e.g. Smith & Hogan, *op. cit.* p. 161 or Glanville Williams, *Criminal Law – the General Part* p. 704.
[149] *Times* 19 and 22 September 1936; 82 L.J. Newsp. 310
[150] 1886 16 Cox CC 355.
[151] But there is some doubt as to whether anti-semitism is covered by the provisions on incitement to racial hatred: see Lester and Bindman, *Race and Law* (Penguin 1972) p. 363.
[152] 30 Cr App R 57.
[153] 1954 1 QB 158.

been adequately discussed above under the heading of conspiracy to corrupt public morals. If offences against public morals form a separate type of conspiracy, and it will be argued below that they do, then the public mischief umbrella was unnecessary.

Bhagwan (1970)[154] was a Commonwealth immigrant who came to England clandestinely in 1967. He landed on a deserted beach and so avoided encountering an immigration officer within 24 hours of his arrival. Under the immigration laws as they then stood he could not be refused admission unless, within 24 hours of landing, he had been required by an immigration officer to submit to an examination. By avoiding such examination he obtained the right to remain in England permanently; and the manner of his landing did not become a statutory offence until the passing of the Commonwealth Immigrants Act 1968. The prosecution conceded that he had committed no statutory offence; and so he was charged, not actually with conspiracy to effect a public mischief, but with conspiracy to evade the control on immigration imposed under the Commonwealth Immigrants Act 1962. His counsel contended that this was not an offence known to the law; and this contention was upheld by the Court of Appeal and the House of Lords. The public mischief charge should not be used by the courts to plug loopholes left in the law by Parliament, 'unless the means adopted are unlawful or the prejudice likely to be caused falls within one of the established categories of public mischief held by previous decisions as so contrary to public policy to justify penal sanctions'.[155]

Knuller (1972) followed *Shaw*; the *ratio* was limited to conspiracy to corrupt public morals, and the defendants could probably have been convicted on a charge of procuring under s.4 of the Sexual Offences Act 1967.[156]

The next reported case is *Foy*,[157] which followed *Porter*[158] in holding that an agreement to indemnify bail constitutes a public mischief; but as in *Porter* the defendants could probably have been convicted for contempt of court. The Court of Appeal also upheld the ruling in *Porter* and in *Brailsford* that the question of what is a public mischief is a question of law for the judge, and not a question of fact to be left to the jury.

In May 1973 there appeared the peculiar case of *Hunter*,[159] in which three youths had been indulging in what the report describes as horseplay with a girl, as a result of which she died. They hid her body under a pile of paving stones. The Court of Appeal quashed their convictions for manslaughter, but held that they had rightly been con-

154 1970 3 All ER 97.
155 *per* Lord Diplock, 1970 3 All ER at 105.
156 *per* Lord Diplock, 1972 3 WLR at 171.
157 1972 Crim LR 504.
158 *supra*.
159 1973 3 WLR 374.

victed of conspiracy to prevent the burial of a corpse. The Court relied on the ancient precedent of *Young* (1780)[160] cited in *Russell on Crime*[161] as support for the proposition that to prevent the burial of a dead body is an indictable misdemeanour; and in agreeing with *Russell* that prevention of burial is an offence the Court clearly treated the case as an agreement to commit a crime.

Finally among the public mischief cases must now be listed *Kamara*,[162] which was treated as a conspiracy to commit a tort at first instance and in the Court of Appeal; but in the House of Lords Lord Hailsham, after mentioning a dozen of the cases discussed above, concluded:

> 'A combination to commit a public mischief can be indictable. The categories here are not closed, and I have no doubt that they include a combination to trespass upon or occupy a foreign Embassy or a Commonwealth High Commission, the inviolability of which Her Majesty's Government are under an obligation to protect. I feel certain, too, that there are many other public buildings owned by the authorities in this country to which the same considerations would apply.'[163]

Any conspiracy to commit a tort, therefore, which becomes criminal because it involves the public interest is also a conspiracy to effect a public mischief; and for that reason *Kamara* has been classified among the Public Security cases in the table set out on page 49 below.

There remain the unreported cases, *i.e.* cases which did not find their way into the Law Reports. We know something about these cases from two sources: from information kindly supplied by the Director of Public Prosecutions, and from the newspapers. In June 1972 the Attorney-General informed the House of Commons that 16 prosecutions for conspiracy to effect a public mischief had been brought since 1962;[164] and in answer to a private inquiry the D.P.P. revealed that these prosecutions were preferred in relation to the following circumstances:

1. Inciting a person to indemnify bail.[165]
2. Using false documents in order to obtain passports, and in order to secure entry into the UK.
3. Making false statements to the police in relation to the identity of a driver.

160 Unreported but referred to in *Lynn* 1788 2 Term Rep 733.
161 12th ed. p. 1420
162 1973 3 WLR 198.
163 *ibid.* at 213.
164 Hansard 26 June 1972.
165 *Foy* 1972 Crim. L.R. 504.

4. Making false statements to the police in relation to the disappearance of a relative.
5. Making false statements to the police in relation to the occurrence of a criminal offence.
6. The removal of possible evidence by trespassers.
7. Making false alarm messages to the military and to fire brigades.
8. Making a false statement as to the medical condition of a close relative in order to secure compassionate release from prison.
9. Using a radio device for the disruption of police communications.
10. Using CS gas to disrupt proceedings in Parliament.[166]
11. Causing public alarm by the use of imitation explosives in the street.[167]
12. Causing public alarm by the use of imitation explosives in a post office.
13. Causing public alarm by the use of imitation explosives in a telephone kiosk.
14. Impersonating central and local government employees in order to trace debtors.[167a]
15. Misuse of public position in order to secure private gain.
16. Unlawfully procuring a potentially poisonous fluid intended for prisoners in Wormwood Scrubs.

Without having further information it is impossible to comment on these cases in any detail; but several of them seem to provide a basis for substantive charges rather than an indictment for conspiracy to effect a public mischief. (2) appears to be a case of forgery, (3) (4) and (5) might justify a charge under the Police Act 1964 s.51 (3),[168] (6) appears to be a case of conspiracy to pervert the course of justice, (10) probably involves an offence against The Explosive Substances Act 1883 or the Offences Against the Person Act 1861; (11) might be prosecuted under The Explosives Act 1875 s.79 and s.80, if the Act covers imitation explosives, (12) and (13) might with the same proviso be offences under the Post Office Act 1953 s.60, (15) probably contravenes the Prevention of Corruption Act 1906 and (16) would also seem to give rise to a charge under the Offences Against the Person Act 1861.

As for the public mischief cases which have been given publicity in the newspapers, all the recent prosecutions are cases involving explosives and arising out of the troubles in Ireland. The precedent for bringing public mischief charges in this type of case appears to be the prosecution of Lieutenant Twisleton-Wykeham-Fiennes, who in 1966

[166] *Roche & Bowes Egan* The *Times* February 18 1971.
[167] Presumably this is *T.-W.-Fiennes*; but the explosives in his possession appear to have been genuine – see The *Times* October 6 1966.
[167a] *Cf. Withers* 1974 2 WLR 26.
[168] But see *Rice v Connolly* 1966 3 WLR 17.

was convicted of conspiracy to cause a public mischief[169] when he and some friends let off explosives in Castle Combe, Wiltshire, as a protest against a film company working there. Twisleton-Wykeham-Fiennes and one other also pleaded guilty to a substantive offence of possessing explosives. In *Roche and Bowes Egan,*[170] a prosecution brought for throwing CS gas in the House of Commons, the judge sought to mitigate the effect of the conspiracy charge by directing the jury that intent to commit a specific crime must be established before they could convict; and Bowes Egan was acquitted.

The trial of *de Faoit, O'Sullivan and others*[171] also contained a charge of conspiracy to effect a public mischief, in addition to charges of conspiracy to possess firearms and ammunition and unlawfully possessing firearms. On the fourth day of the trial the prosecution case was withdrawn and the judge directed the jury to find the defendants not guilty. They had been in prison awaiting trial for 8 months.

Finally in the Aldershot Bomb trial, *Jenkinson and others,*[172] the public mischief charge reached its ultimate absurdity. Seven people had died and the first seven counts on the indictment were charges of murder. The other counts related to the possession of firearms, explosives and ammunition, and there was one count of conspiracy to pervert the course of justice; but count 9 on the indictment charged the murderers with conspiracy to effect a public mischief. The judge directed the jury to return a verdict of not guilty on that charge.

(c) *The Categories of Conspiracy*

Clear thinking in conspiracy cases has frequently been obfuscated because the categories of conspiracy are too broadly defined. The classification which follows is an attempt to define the various categories of criminal conspiracy in a way which is historically correct, and it is based on the analyses in *Russell on Crime,*[173] Harrison[174] and Lord Diplock's speech in *Knuller.*[175]

The classification is very close to being a statement of what, in 1973, the law of conspiracy is, but not quite: it takes little account, for instance, of Lord Hailsham's speech in *Kamara*[176] – a classic example of blurring the different categories. Rather it is a statement of what, *on the authorities,* the law should be. The three broad categories adopted in the foregoing analysis will be repeated, but the last two categories will be broken down into more detailed heads of conspiracy.

169 *Times* October 6 1966.
170 *Times* February 18 1971; New Law Journal April 8 1971.
171 *Guardian* 13 June 1972.
172 *Times* 17 October – 15 November 1972 *passim.*
173 12th Edition vol. 2 pp. 1475–1490.
174 *Conspiracy as a Crime and as a Tort,* London 1924, pp. 146–148.
175 1972 3 WLR at 165–169.
176 1973 3 WLR 198.

I. *Conspiracy to commit a crime*

Russell pp. 1475–8; Harrison p. 146 para (3); Lord Diplock 166F–167H ('the second stream').

This category is straightforward, and may conveniently be made to include conspiracies expressly prohibited by statute (classified separately by Harrison).

II. *Conspiracy to defraud or injure a private individual*

Russell pp. 1481–4 paras. 1 and 2, 1485 and 1488–90; Harrison pp. 146 paras. (1) and (4), and 147 para. (6); Lord Diplock 166A–166F.

1. *Injury to an individual by misuse of the process of the courts*

Russell pp. 1481–4 paras. 1 and 2; Harrison p. 146 para. (1); Lord Diplock 166A–166C.

This head originates in the old Ordinances of Conspiracy,[177] and having been only gradually extended it now comprises *part* of the modern conspiracy to pervert the course of justice.

2. *Injury to an individual by fraud or deceit*

Russell p. 1485; Harrison p. 146 para. (4); Lord Diplock 168H–169E.

Russell and Lord Diplock seem to doubt whether this is distinct from the category of frauds on the public.[178] Harrison's view that it *is* distinct is supported by:

(a) the reasoning of Lord Mansfield C.J. in *Wheatley,*[179] quoted by Lord Diplock in *Knuller.*[180]

(b) *R. v. Fountain.*[181]

3. *Economic injury to an individual in his trade or office*

Russell p. 1488 *et seq*; Harrison p. 147 para. (6) and see pp. 118–20; Lord Diplock 166C–166E.

In the nineteenth century the cases in this category were exclusively trade union cases. The category is now probably obsolete as a result of statutory intervention in the field of industrial relations.[182] The cases led to the development of the civil remedy of conspiracy, and they also merge into the next category.

4. *Injury to individuals other than in their economic capacity*

Russell pp. 1488–90; Harrison p. 147 para. (6); Lord Diplock

[177] See chapter 2.
[178] Dealt with in (iii) (3) below.
[179] 1761 2 Burr 1125.
[180] 1972 3 WLR at 168G.
[181] 1965 2 All ER 671.
[182] See chapter 2.

168H–169B. This is the most controversial category in (II), the authority for much of its scope resting only on *dicta*. Its existence was the central question in *Kamara* and in *Hain*. The category does not include all agreements to commit a tort; but it may also extend beyond them to include agreements to do acts which are non-tortious. Before *Kamara* agreements to commit torts were considered indictable only when they involved fraud or malice[183] or in some way threatened the public interest;[184] but there was some authority that conspiracies involving a malicious or deliberate interference with the 'rights' of individuals were indictable, even if such interferences did not amount to tortious misconduct.[185] An example is *Willetts* (1906),[186] where the defendants were charged with pirating copyright music (not in itself a criminal offence) and the Common Serjeant said: 'For people to combine together to deprive a man of his civil rights generally comes within the definition of a criminal conspiracy'.[187]

III. *Conspiracy to produce a public mischief*

Russell pp. 1478–88; Harrison pp. 146–7 para. (5); Lord Diplock 168A–169G.

In many of the cases in this group the words 'public mischief' were never used. The categories are all independent heads of conspiracy in their own right, the only connection between them being that they all involve an element of harm to the public. Nevertheless a number of cases will fall into more than one category; and furthermore conspiracies to injure individuals often overlap with conspiracies containing a public element, *e.g.* Kamara. Finally it should be remembered that many of the 'public mischief' cases themselves also involved agreements to commit crimes;[188] but while that may obviate the need for a generic head of conspiracy labelled 'public mischief', it does not disprove its undoubted existence at the present time.

1. *Acts contrary to public morals or public decency*

Russell pp. 1479–80; Harrison p. 146 para. (5) (a); Lord Diplock 169G–170B.

Lord Diplock in *Knuller* argued that this category does not exist, but he was in a 4:1 minority; and so was Lord Reid when he put forward a similar argument in *Shaw*.

[183] For the meaning of which see 'Conspiring to Squat' 1971 Crim LR 342 344–6.

[184] *Bramley* 11 Journal of Criminal Law 36; Lord Bramwell in *Mogul Steamship* 1892 AC at 48; Lord Hailsham in *Kamara* 1973 3 WLR 198.

[185] *E.g.* Lord Diplock in *Bhagwan* 1972 AC 60 at 79G.

[186] 70 JP 127.

[187] For other authorities see the cases cited by Lord Hailsham in *Kamara*: Lord Halsbury in *Mogul Steamship* 1892 AC at 38 (combination to insult and annoy is criminal), Lord Simon in the *Crofter* case 1942 AC 435, Lord Brampton in *Quinn v Leathem* 1901 AC 495, *Parnell* etc.

[188] The cases are discussed in detail on pages 38–45 above.

2. *Perverting the course of justice*

Russell pp. 1484–5 para. 3; Harrison p. 147 para. (5) (b); Lord Diplock 166C.

Lord Diplock and Lord Hailsham in *Kamara*, seem to assimilate this category with injury to individuals by misuse of legal process (II (1) above) but the two are factually and legally distinct: compare Harrison para. (1) and para. (5) (b).

3. *Cheats and frauds on the public at large*

Russell pp. 1485–8; Harrison p. 147 para. (5) (c); Lord Diplock 168F–169G.

Again Lord Diplock assimilates this category with frauds and deceits against an individual, but they are quite distinctly treated in the cases. The essence of the public cheat is the public nature of the cheat involved, and no particular victim need be contemplated by the conspirators (e.g. *de Berenger*).[189]

4. *Fraud and corruption against government departments*

Russell pp. 1476, 1485; Harrison p. 147 para. (5) (c); Lord Diplock 169B–169E.

This may be a sub-category of (3); Harrison treats it as such, but Lord Diplock considers it to be distinct (169B).

5. *Acts against public order and security*

Russell p. 1485; Harrison p. 147 para. (5) (d).

This category is not mentioned by Lord Diplock; and indeed when Harrison classified it separately most of the cases he cited – *e.g. Starling*[190] and *O'Connell*[191] – were easily explicable on other grounds. But recently the public mischief charge has become popular in cases involving explosives – *Twisleton-Wykeham-Fiennes* (1966),[192] the *CS gas* case[192] in the House of Commons (1971), the Aldershot bomb trial (1972) and the trial of *de Faoit and others* (1972),[192] so that its separate existence is now probably established.

[189] 1814 3 M & S 67.
[190] 1663 1 Sid 174.
[191] 1844 1 Cl & F 155.
[192] *supra* page 45.

We are now in a position to classify the cases on public mischief in a simple table. The actual 'public mischief' cases, i.e. cases in which the words 'conspiracy to commit a public mischief' are used either in the indictment or in the judgment, are underlined: it will be seen that they are fairly evenly distributed across all five categories.

Public Morals	Pervert Justice	Public Cheats	Govt. departments	Public Security
Lord Grey 1682	MacDaniel 1756	*de Berenger* 1814	Starling 1665	Murphy 1837
Thorp 1696	Mawby 1796	Hilbers 1818	Daniell 1704	Vincent 1839
Delaval 1763	Steventon 1802	Esdaile 1858	Edwards 1725	Shellard 1839
Young 1780	Locker 1804	Lewis 1869	Vertue v Clive 1769	O'Connell 1844
Mears 1851	Wade 1814	Gurney 1869	Vaughan 1760	(Mulcahy 1868)
Howell 1864	Kroehl 1818	Aspinall 1875	Compton 1783	Parnell 1881
Saunders 1875	Thomas 1824	Scott v Brown 1892	*Higgins* 1801	*Leese* 1936
Mackenzie 1910	Bushell 1826	Parker 1916	Pollman 1809	*T-W-Fiennes* 1966
Berg 1927	Hamp 1852	*Newland* 1954	Seward 1834	*Roche* 1971
Shaw 1962	Tibbits 1902		*Brailsford* 1905	*Aldershot case* 1972
Knuller 1972	*Porter* 1910		Whitaker 1915	*de Faoit* 1972
	Meyrick 1929		*Bassey* 1931	*Kamara* 1973
	Sharp 1938		*Young* 1944	
	Foy 1972		Owen 1957	
			Bhagwan 1972	

Three caveats should be given in relation to this table:

1. none of the columns contains an exhaustive list
2. each case is only listed in one column, but several cases have a claim to be mentioned in more than one column
3. the classification of many of the old cases can only be tentative because of inadequate reports.

However one conclusion is overwhelming, and that is that the head of 'conspiracy to effect a public mischief' is not properly a category of conspiracy[193] at all, but rather conceals five separate categories of conspiracy which have (in varying degrees) good historical claims to be categories in their own right.

[193] Although at the moment it can properly be charged as the Statement of Offence in an indictment, provided that as a matter of law the Particulars justify it.

D

4. DEFECTS OF THE PRESENT LAW: THE SUBSTANTIVE LAW

> 'A doctrine so vague in its outlines and uncertain in its fundamental nature as criminal conspiracy lends no strength or glory to the law; it is a veritable quicksand of shifting opinion and ill-considered thought'.[194]

In this chapter the law will be criticized in the framework of the traditional classification of conspiracy.

I. *Agreements to commit a crime*

There can be no very strong objections to this head of conspiracy unless one wishes to abolish conspiracy altogether as an inchoate offence. There is however one significant defect in the present law, and that is the rule that conspiracies to commit summary offences are themselves *indictable* offences.

Of this rule Professor Glanville Williams has said,

> 'In this respect conspiracy seems to be unique among the inchoate crimes, for ... the better view is that the crimes of incitement and attempt are possible only in respect of indictable offences.'[195]

Unfortunately this is no longer true, at least with regard to incitement. The Magistrates' Courts Act 1952 provides that an incitement to commit a summary offence may be dealt with summarily with the consent of the accused; and in *Curr*[196] the Court of Appeal came to the inescapable conclusion that incitement to commit a summary offence is indictable. The rule with regard to attempt is still undecided; probably attempt is still possible only in respect of indictable offences.

However the decision in *Curr*, although unavoidable in the face of the Statute, *must* be wrong both in logic and in policy: the mere solicitation of an offence cannot be regarded as more serious than the actual commission of that offence. And *a fortiori* with regard to attempt. Nor, it is submitted, can a combination to commit a summary

[194] Sayre 1922 Harv LR 393.
[195] *op. cit* p. 686.
[196] 1967 1 All ER 478.

offence be regarded as a greater social danger than its actual commission. In the words of R. S. Wright,[197] summary offences

'are not in themselves of grave enough consequence to be matters for indictment; and, if so, it must in general be immaterial whether the results are produced by one person or by two or more persons. To permit two persons to be indicted for a conspiracy to make a slide in the street of a town, or to catch hedge sparrows in April, would be to destroy that distinction between crimes and minor offences which in every country it is held important to preserve'.

The draft Criminal Code produced by the Royal Commission in 1879 in essence limited conspiracy to agreements to commit indictable offences; and one of the Amendments moved by Baroness Birk[198] in the House of Lords debate on the 1972 Criminal Justice Bill would have had the same effect.

At the very least a conspiracy to commit a summary offence should only be triable summarily. If it is felt that certain summary offences are greatly aggravated when committed in combination, as Lord Widgery argued in the House of Lords debate,[199] then aggravated penalties should be provided by statute for such cases. This again was the opinion of R. S. Wright:

'There can be very few kinds of minor offences, the quality of which can be so altered by agreement as to make it necessary to punish them by indictment; and those kinds ought to be considered beforehand by the legislature and specified in the written law.'[200]

But if the rule with regard to attempt is that attempt cannot be committed in relation to summary offences, then it should be considered whether that rule should not apply to conspiracy also; in which case this head of conspiracy would be limited to agreements to commit indictable offences – as both the 1879 draft Code and Lady Birk recommended.

II. *Agreements to commit a tort*

Part of the judgment of the Court of Appeal in *Kamara*[201] is set out on page 22 above. The *ratio decidendi* of Lawton L.J. may be reduced to a simple syllogism: a conspiracy is an agreement to do an unlawful act; a tort is commonly held to be an unlawful act; therefore any agreement to commit a tort is a criminal conspiracy. Nowhere is the

[197] *op. cit* p. 83.
[198] Amendment 37 Hansard 24 July 1972.
[199] Hansard 24 July 1972 cols 1117–1118.
[200] *op. cit* p. 85.
[201] 1972 3 All ER 999.

power of Lord Denman's magic jingle, and its paralysing effect on judicial thought-processes, more glaringly displayed; the blatant begging of the question (what does 'unlawful' mean in the definition of conspiracy?) and the rigid conceptualism of the answer, so alien to the empirical tradition of the common law, made the judgment appear to be almost deliberately provocative.[202] It never occurrred to Wright, writing 100 years ago, that 'unlawful' in this context might include *every* tortious act:

> 'for not only is there the express authority of *Turner*'s case (1811), which has never been questioned on this point, to the contrary effect; but it would be against common sense to hold criminal an agreement between two persons to walk in a park without leave, or to dishonour a bill'.[203]

Fortunately in the House of Lords[204] some measure of common sense was restored. *Turner*[205] was put in its proper place, the Denman formula was examined and found not to be an all-inclusive definition, and the House made a brave attempt to define which agreements to commit a tort are criminal and which are not. In doing so the Lords fully recognized how difficult a task they were setting themselves, and how much simpler it would be from the conceptual point of view to decide either that all agreements to commit a tort are criminal (as the Court of Appeal had held) or that none are (as the Appellants had argued). In the words of Lord Hailsham,

> '. . . [B]oth of the extreme views, namely, that contended for by Sir Dingle Foot for the Appellants and that adopted by the Court of Appeal have manifest attractions from the point of view of simplicity. The intermediate view contended for by Counsel for the Respondent [*i.e.* the prosecution], indeed any view consistent with authority and intermediate between the two extremes, presents great difficulties of definition, principle and application'.[206]

It will be argued here that the difficulties of definition, principle and application are so great that both the tests proposed by Lord Hailsham contain fatal flaws. Each test will be examined in turn.

1. *Intention to inflict more than nominal damage*

> '. . . [A] combination the execution of which has as its object not merely a tort or other actionable wrong, but also . . . the intention to

[202] The decision was not only wrong in principle, it went quite against the balance of the authorities: see page 25, and the proper treatment accorded to *Turner* in the House of Lords.
[203] *op. cit* p. 66.
[204] 1973 3 WLR 198.
[205] 13 East 228, 104 ER 357.
[206] 1973 3 WLR at 206.

inflict on its victim injury and damage which goes beyond the field of the nominal is indictable . . .'[207]

This test of *intention* has already played a significant part in the development of civil conspiracy, and indeed one half of the cases cited by Lord Hailsham as authority for his proposition that the defendants' intention may make their tortious action criminal are in fact cases of civil rather than criminal conspiracy. In the civil law extreme difficulty has been experienced in conspiracy cases in the application of any test based on intention, because of the impossibility of assessing in a sufficiently judicial manner what was the defendants' 'predominant motive'. The famous trio of cases before the House of Lords, *Mogul Steamship*,[208] *Allen v. Flood*[209] and *Quinn v. Leathem*[210] show just how unsatisfactory the test is: the decisions are not worth trying to reconcile.

Of course it may be that the predominant motive doctrine will not be imported into the criminal test (indeed, this is implied by Lord Hailsham in his second formulation of the *ratio decidendi*, on p. 217); but if no attempt is made to distinguish between the different intentions which motivate conspirators, then the House of Lords may inadvertently have spread the criminal net wider than it intended. For Lord Hailsham intended his test to apply to other torts beside trespass:

> '. . . whether the object be achieved by trespass to land, goods or person, by ruin of the reputation through the defamation of character, by the commission of private nuisance, by some contrivance of fraud, by the imposition of force, or by any other means which is tortious'.[211]

If we apply the test to private nuisance, some startling results emerge. Suppose a company instals a new furnace which the directors know will increase the quantity of smoke coming out of their factory, but they think that the level of pollution will still be tolerable and the risk is worth taking. They are sued in private nuisance by a neighbouring householder, who is granted an injunction ordering the company to cut down on the amount of smoke emitted. Are the police now to prosecute the directors of the company for conspiracy? 'The execution of the combination necessarily involves and is known and intended to involve the infliction on its victim of something more than nominal damage'[212]; if the damage had been nominal the neighbours

[207] *per* Lord Hailsham, *ibid* at **216**.
[208] 1892 AC 25.
[209] 1898 AC 1.
[210] 1901 AC 495.
[211] 1973 3 WLR at 216–7.
[212] *per* Lord Hailsham, 1973 3 WLR at 217.

would not have been granted an injunction. And if it is argued that the intention of the directors was not so much to cause damage to their neighbour as to increase their profits, then that introduces the predominant motive test; and it could equally be argued that the intention of the demonstrators in *Kamara* was not so much to cause damage to the occupiers of the High Commission as to win publicity for their cause (the father of at least one of them was under sentence of death at the time). It was doubtless with these difficulties in mind that the Court of Appeal observed:

> 'If conspirators' intents had to be considered, judges and juries would almost certainly find themselves struggling with the casuist problems of greater or lesser evils, maybe with the same kind of results as were ridiculed by Pascal.'[213]

It might also be argued that the prosecuting authorities can be expected to use their good sense in deciding when to prosecute; but this is no safeguard because it *invites* the authorities to be discriminatory in the exercise of their discretion[214] – and where the authorities choose not to prosecute there is nothing to prevent a private prosecution from being brought, *Hain* being a recent example. As Lord Reid observed in *Knuller*,

> 'It may be said that no prosecution would ever be brought except in a very bad case. But I have expressed on previous occasions my opinion that a bad law is not defensible on the ground that it will be judiciously administered.'[215]

The fundamental objection to an open-ended law of this kind is that the authorities inevitably lay themselves open to allegations of unfair discrimination in selecting victims for prosecution, and those victims – squatters, demonstrators, pickets and the like – will be tempted to see in legal decisions merely the prejudice of a certain social class, or of the government of the day. As the *Times* remarked in its editorial on the case,

> 'The decision of the House of Lords in *Kamara v. D.P.P.* does little to clear up the inherently confusing state of the laws of conspiracy or indeed to allay the fears of those who believe that these laws are being increasingly used against persons involved in protest of a political or civil liberties nature.'[216]

[213] 1972 3 All ER at 1005.
[214] A discretion with which the courts will not interfere: see *Blackburn v Metropolitan Police Commissioner*, *Times* Law Report November 27 1972, and Wilcox: *The Decision to Prosecute* (1972).
[215] 1972 3 WLR at 150.
[216] *Times* 5 July 1973.

So long as the courts continue to provide justification for such beliefs popular respect for the law and its administration by the courts will tend to diminish.

The final argument against casuistic tests of this kind and the confrontations they provoke is that both are *unnecessary*. Lord Hailsham himself admitted this when he said

> 'I have little doubt that a combination to commit trespass in such a manner as to break the statutes of forcible entry and detainer is a criminal conspiracy, and though this was not the course taken here, I have little doubt but that it could have been taken here, and could be taken in the vast majority of the squatting cases, or the "sit in" cases, or many of the cases in which sports grounds are forcibly occupied or disrupted.'[217]

That being the case, squatters and demonstrators *etc.* should be prosecuted for the substantive offences they have committed, or for conspiracy or incitement to commit those offences, but not for the nebulous new offence of conspiracy to commit a trespass with intent to inflict more than nominal damage.

2. *Invasion of the public domain*

It was noted in chapter 3 that this formula can only be another version of the public interest test, which was expressed in a more familiar form by Lord Cross of Chelsea when he said:

> 'An agreement by several to commit acts which if done by one would only amount to a tort may constitute a criminal conspiracy if, as has been said, "the public has a sufficient interest".'[218]

This test also has a certain pedigree in the law of conspiracy, and it was recognized earlier that if certain combinations to commit torts are to be criminal, then the 'public interest' test is a sensible limitation of criminality: for criminal sanctions should only be invoked in cases of injury to the public, and not merely where some private right is infringed. But the questions to be asked now are:

(a) Can the test ever be made sufficiently certain?

(b) Is a judge the right person to administer the test?

Details of the test were not given by Lord Hailsham, so that the only indication of the sort of criteria the House of Lords had in mind is provided by Lord Cross of Chelsea:

> '... [T]he agreement would have consequences sufficiently harm-

[217] 1973 3 WLR at 213.
[218] *ibid* at 219.

ful to call for penal sanctions . . . because, for example, of the nature of the property on which the trespass was to be committed or of the means to be employed in carrying out the trespass or of the object to be achieved by it'.

The same sort of test was applied in the trial of Peter Hain. Towards the end of the trial Judge Gillis told counsel:

'I propose to direct the jury in these terms; Where two or more persons combine together – agree together – intending deliberately to deprive other persons of their legal rights, or to infringe them or to interfere with, or to prevent the exercise of such legal rights, on matters of substantial public interest, by unlawful means of substantial public concern, such combination is, in my opinion, a criminal conspiracy indictable by Common Law that is triable by a jury . . . I shall inform the jury that "substantial public interest", in the sense in which I have employed that term, means matters, activities, of real interest to the public, and "substantial public concern" means matters of real importance to the public; something of importance to citizens who are interested in the maintenance of law and order as something that goes beyond the mere dispute of one person against another.'[219]

In giving this direction Judge Gillis was relying heavily on the direction to the jury given by Stable J. in *Bramley* (1946).[220] That was an early squatting case in which five defendants who had been running a campaign to house homeless families were charged *inter alia* with conspiracy to trespass and conspiracy to incite others to commit trespass. Stable J. directed the jury in these words:

'If, members of the jury, you are satisfied that this combination to infringe the rights of the owners of these flats, having regard to the scope of the combination itself as disclosed in the evidence, and having regard to the magnitude of the common aim which it is sought to achieve, and to the numbers involved, and the methods adopted to give effect to that common aim – if you think that having regard to all those circumstances as disclosed in the evidence, this matter resolves itself into something which transcends that sphere where the property owner aggrieved can go to the civil court and claim an injunction for damages or whatever it may be, and passes into that sphere where it becomes a matter of public concern for citizens who are interested in the maintenance of good order – if you

[219] Transcript, 8 August 1972.
[220] 1946 Journal of Criminal Law 36.

think that this case comes into that category, a matter not merely of private rights or private interests, but a matter of vital public concern, I say that a combination of persons, albeit no criminal act contemplated, intended or planned or committed, and that all that was done, intended or planned was the infringement of a private right or private rights, then you should convict.'[221]

The test as laid down in *Kamara* and in *Bramley* is a great deal more detailed than that offered to the jury in *Hain*. The test in *Hain* – 'something of importance to citizens who are interested in the maintenance of law and order . . .' – is hopelessly vague and must be regarded as inadequate. The test in *Kamara* requires the judge to have regard to the nature of the property, the means employed, and the object to be achieved by the trespass; *Bramley* adds the magnitude of the common aim and the numbers involved. Although more detailed, it might be doubted whether these tests are sufficiently certain to ensure that like cases will be treated alike.

There is much more chance of this, however, since the House of Lords ruled in *Kamara* that the question of whether a trespass involves the public interest is a question of law for the judge, and not, as Stable J. had suggested in *Bramley,* a question of fact for the jury.

'It is for the judge to decide as a matter of law whether the circumstances alleged in the indictment are sufficient if proved to the satisfaction of the jury to render the agreement to commit the act or acts in question a criminal offence' (*per* Lord Cross of Chelsea).[222]

But is a judge competent to do this? And in particular, is he competent to adjudicate on whether the 'object to be achieved' by the trespass adds to or detracts from the criminality of the offence? In effect, the judge is being asked to define the boundaries of the criminal law with regard to this particular offence. The Court of Appeal in *Kamara* was well aware of this difficulty:

'If the public interest is to be considered, as counsel for the Crown suggested, who is to decide what it is? The judge? Or the jury? Are either competent? Should evidence be admitted on this issue? If not, why not? If the judge is to decide, he may well take the verdict from the jury; if the jury is to decide, part of the law of conspiracy can be stated in four words : "*salus populi, suprema lex*".'[223]

These objections must be regarded as fundamental. Neither judge nor

[221] *Hain* Transcript, 8 August 1972.
[222] 1973 3 WLR at 219.
[223] 1972 3 All ER at 1005.

jury is competent to decide what is in the public interest; nor are they competent to draw the line between what is the concern of the criminal law and what is not. Adjudication on these questions is essentially a legislative function, and legislative functions should be left to our elected representatives in Parliament. In particular the enforcement of public order should not be a question for juries, being the concern of the Executive; but in *Bramley* as in *Hain* the combination becomes criminal when the defendant's conduct 'passes into that sphere where it becomes a matter of public concern for citizens who are interested in the maintenance of good order'. At the annual general meeting of *Justice* in 1972 Lord Devlin had this to say of the connection between law and order:

> 'I think that law and order is a very unfortunate conjunction of words because they signify for this purpose two things that are quite different. The judges are responsible for the maintenance of the law; the Executive is responsible for the maintenance of order. Order may spring from the law, but law and order coupled like that as if one body or one person had to enforce both gives a wholly misleading idea of what the judges ought to be doing.'[224]

The conclusion must be that any definition of the scope of conspiracy which depends upon an application of the public interest test is an unacceptable definition. The Court of Appeal in *Kamara* felt the force of this objection and widened the definition; but it is equally possible, as the House of Lords recognized, to narrow the definition so that agreements to commit torts are excluded altogether. The number of reported prosecutions brought for conspiracy to commit a tort, apart from conspiracies to defraud and the industrial cases of the nineteenth century, is so small that it can hardly be argued that this category of conspiracy is essential for the protection of people's rights. If it is felt that society requires protection from conduct such as that in *Hain*, then that protection must be provided by Parliament (as in the Conspiracy and Protection of Property Act 1875, the origin of one of the charges used against Hain).[225] It is constitutionally improper for the courts unilaterally to provide such protection, and their error is compounded when they do so by arrogating to themselves the right to sit in judgment on the political methods and objects of others, when those methods and objects are not in themselves criminal offences.

[224] Quoted by Lord Gardiner in the House of Lords, Hansard 27 July 1972 col 1562.
[225] Not expressly; but part of the particulars on the first count of the indictment charged him with 'watching and besetting places where members of the team happened to be, persistently following members of the team from place to place', etc. – words taken from s. 7(4) and (5).

III. *The third head*

Conspiracy to corrupt public morals

The wealth of literature which has arisen attacking the decision of the House of Lords in *Shaw*[226] makes it unnecessary to reiterate the criticisms of this area of the law except in the barest outline. But the decision in *Knuller,* while remedying some of the defects of *Shaw,* has confirmed or even added to the others. The offence of conspiracy to corrupt public morals is still a threat to our civil liberties in the following ways:

1. If *Shaw* represents, as its critics claim, an exercise in judicial legislation, then in that case and in all the prosecutions for conspiracy to corrupt public morals since then, the charge used was one which had simply been found convenient by the judges in 1961 and which had never been sanctioned by Parliament. To prove this allegation it is necessary briefly to reconsider the controversy whether *Shaw* created the offence of conspiracy to corrupt public morals, or whether that offence had previously existed at common law. It will be argued here that even if one accepts the House of Lords' ruling that the offence had at one time existed at common law, nevertheless there was an element of creation in holding that the offence did *still* exist.

The *ratio decidendi* in *Shaw* was twofold. The majority held, in the words of Lord Simon of Glaisdale in *Knuller*

> 'that not only was the offence of conspiracy to corrupt public morals established as a matter of continuous legal history in English law, but also that it was desirable that this should be so'.[227]

This second element in the decision was essential in order to distinguish offences against public morals from the other 'unravished remnants of the common law'[228] which would otherwise by implication be revived at the same time. How else could the House of Lords distinguish between conspiracy to corrupt morals and similarly fossilized offences like blasphemy, except by making a value judgment as to which of the old offences still had utility, and which were now obsolete?
In the words of Viscount Simonds,

> 'The law must be related to the changing standards of life, not yielding to every shifting impulse of the popular will but having regard to fundamental assessments of human values and the pur-

[226] 1962 AC 220. For adverse comment see 1961 CLJ 144, 75 Harv LR 1652, 24 MLR 626; by far the best criticism is contained in 1964 42 Can Bar R 561, where the historical background and the constitutional implications are thoroughly explored. For a discussion of the moral issues involved see Hart: *Law, Liberty and Morality*. For a defence of *Shaw* see Goodhart, 77 LQR 560.
[227] 1972 3 WLR at 179–180.
[228] *per* Viscount Simonds, 1961 2 All ER at 453.

poses of society. Today a denial of the fundamental Christian doctrine, which in past centuries would have been regarded by the ecclesiastical courts as heresy and by the common law as blasphemy, will no longer be an offence if the decencies of controversy are observed.'[229]

Lord Diplock makes this point in *Knuller*:

'Nor do I think that it was open to the House in *Shaw*'s case to select some particular field of mischief in which the power of the judiciary to create new crimes survives. The general statement to be found in the cases up to the first part of the nineteenth century as to why the judges thought fit to punish some particular kind of conduct if they justify anything justify too much. If these are to be the authority for what was done in *Shaw*'s case they must likewise be authority for a general power to punish any conduct which the court considers injurious to the public.'[230]

Now however the second part of the *ratio decidendi* in *Shaw* has been dropped. It was expressed at its strongest by Viscount Simonds in such assertions as

'In the sphere of criminal law, I entertain no doubt that there remains in the courts of law a residual power to enforce the supreme and fundamental purpose of the law, to conserve not only the safety and order but also the moral welfare of the state . . .'

This doctrine, which amounts in effect to a defence of judicial law-making, was abandoned by the House of Lords in *Bhagwan* and in *Knuller*. The judicial retreat from the Simonds doctrine has been described above;[231] it is well expressed by the headnote in *Knuller*:

'*Per curiam*. The decision in *Shaw* is in no way to be taken as lending any support to the doctrine that the courts have some general or residual power either to create new offences or so to widen existing offences as to make punishable conduct of a type hitherto not subject to punishment.'[232]

While recognizing this retreat, and welcoming it, it is important to remember that in *Shaw* the judges' 'general or residual power' to legislate was undoubtedly exercised, as it had to be, in order to dis-

[229] 1961 2 All ER at 452.
[230] 1972 3 WLR at 165.
[231] on pages 36–7, *supra*.
[232] 1972 3 WLR at 144. The words are essentially those of Lord Reid.

criminate between those unravished remnants of the common law which were still considered by the House of Lords to be of value (like conspiracy to corrupt public morals) and those which were not (like blasphemy).[233] This may be thought unimportant, now that the offence of conspiracy to corrupt public morals has undoubtedly passed into our law; but the manner of its entry is relevant to the 40 prosecutions for conspiracy to corrupt public morals which have been brought since *Shaw*. In the forceful words of Bernard Levin, 'it suggests that the prosecuting authorities are using this handy, and preposterously vague, charge wholesale to convict people who have done nothing unlawful at all, but who can be caught in the net provided in 1962 by the judges . . .'[234]

2. It has been argued in defence of these prosecutions that although *Shaw* was a questionable exercise in judicial legislation, nevertheless the decision (and hence the charge of conspiracy to corrupt public morals) has since been tacitly approved by Parliament. Lord Simon of Glaisdale used this argument as one reason for not overruling *Shaw* in *Knuller*:

> 'A second particular reason why this is, over and above constitutional convention, in my view, an unsuitable issue for the exercise of your Lordships' law-making powers[235] is that there have been several occasions when Parliament itself had the opportunity, had it wished to avail itself of it, to abrogate the decision in *Shaw v. D.P.P.* – the Obscene Publications Act 1964 . . ., the Sexual Offences Act 1967, and the Criminal Law Act 1968.'[236]

But legislative silence does not necessarily imply Parliamentary approval, as Lord Diplock pointed out:

> 'It is urged that even if the decision in *Shaw*'s case was an improper exercise of legislative power by this House acting in its judicial capacity, it has now been ratified by the legislature itself, because the legislature has allowed ten years to pass without taking steps to overrule it. It seems to me that to infer parliamentary approval from parliamentary inaction is to take an unrealistic view of the pressure of parliamentary time under party government and of the way in which priorities in competing claims for time for legislation are settled. The suggestion that Parliament tacitly

[233] For an elaboration of this argument and an interesting excursus on negative judicial legislation (when udges in effect repeal offences rather than create them) see Brownlie & Williams, 42 Can Bar R 561.
[234] *Times* 22 June 1972.
[235] Lord Simon is referring to the Practice Direction of 1966 which gives the House of Lords power to overrule its own previous decisions.
[236] 1972 3 WLR at 179.

approved *Shaw*'s case by omitting to deal with it when the Obscene Publications Act, 1959, was amended in 1964 has a particularly hollow ring in the light of the disclosure of the assurance given to Parliament by a Law Officer of the Crown in the course of the debates on the amending Bill that a conspiracy to corrupt public morals would not be charged so as to circumvent the statutory defence in section 4 of the Act of 1959 – which was precisely what had been done in *Shaw*'s case.'[237]

3. The assurance given by the Attorney-General provides the third objection to prosecutions for conspiracy to corrupt public morals. Where the conspiracy prosecution relates to a publication (as was the case in *Shaw* and *Knuller*) the publisher of the allegedly corruptive material is denied the opportunity of pleading the special defence provided by s.4 of the Obscene Publications Act 1959. The section provides that no offence is committed 'if it is proved that publication of the article in question is justified as being for the public good on the ground that it is in the interests of science, literature, art or learning, or other objects of general concern'; but this 'public good' defence can only be pleaded if the defendant is prosecuted under the Act, and not if he is charged with the common law offence of conspiracy.

To make matters worse, it should not really be possible to prosecute the publisher of an obscene publication for conspiracy at all, since the Obscene Publications Act prevented prosecutions under the old common law rules of obscene libel by providing in s.2(4) that 'a person publishing an article shall not be proceeded against for an offence at common law consisting of the publication of any matter contained or embodied in the article where it is of the essence of the offence that the matter is obscene'. Shaw pleaded that he could not therefore be charged with conspiracy since the conspiracy relied on was the obscene publication. The House of Lords rejected this plea because, in Lord Tucker's words, the offence of conspiracy 'did not "consist of the publication" of the magazines, it consisted of an agreement to corrupt public morals by means of the magazines which might never have been published'.[238]

This argument is really a quibble, since the Obscene Publications Act defines obscene as that which tends to deprave and corrupt.[239] Lord Reid makes this point in *Knuller*:

> 'The obvious purpose of section 2(4) is to make available, where the essence of the offence is tending to deprave and corrupt, the defences which are set out in the Act. In *Shaw*'s case it was argued

[237] 1972 3 WLR at 170.
[238] 1961 2 All ER at 166.
[239] Obscene Publications Act s.2.

that section 2(4) excluded prosecution for the offence of corrupting public morals. The matter is dealt with by Lord Tucker.... Technically the distinction which he draws is correct but it appears to me to offend against the policy of the Act and if the draftsman of the Act of 1959 had foreseen the decision in *Shaw*'s case he might well have drafted the subsection differently.'[240]

Indeed he might. When Parliament in 1968 passed a similar Act regulating obscenity in the theatre, it included a similar provision precluding proceedings at common law, but in addition that provision expressly excluded prosecutions for conspiracy to corrupt public morals.[241] Why was s.2(4) of the Obscene Publications Act 1959 not phrased in the same way? An examination of the report of the Select Committee and of Hansard shows that nobody ever thought of it – which is not surprising since it was not realized before *Shaw* that there was a general offence of conspiracy to corrupt public morals. The Select Committee did recommend that obscene publications should be added to the list of crimes which cannot be prosecuted without the consent of the Director of Public Prosecutions; but the Government resisted this recommendation, and when the 1959 Bill was before Parliament the clause requiring the consent of the DPP had to be dropped under Governmental pressure. Then in 1964 the House of Commons had a second chance. After loud protests about the possible use of the conspiracy charge in *Shaw* to defeat the purpose of the Obscene Publications Act, the Solicitor-General repeated an assurance to the House 'that a conspiracy to corrupt public morals would not be charged so as to circumvent the statutory defence in subsection (4)'.[242] (The original assurance had been given by the Attorney-General on 20 June 1961 – immediately after the announcement of the judgment of the House of Lords in *Shaw*.)

In the light of the prosecution in *Knuller*, the protection afforded by that assurance is meaningless. Viscount Simonds had said in *Shaw* that it was desirable that the conspiracy charge should be used where it was doubtful whether a conviction of obscenity under the Obscene Publications Act could be obtained;[243] and the prosecution in *Knuller* took him at his word. The result was that in *Knuller* the defendants were unable to raise any 'public good' defence to justify their advertisements. The Attorney-General's Department has suggested that any such defence would be 'fanciful';[244] but Baroness Birk,[245] Bernard Levin[246] and John

[240] 1972 3 WLR at 148.
[241] Theatres Act 1968, s. 2(4).
[242] Hansard, Vol 695, col 1212 3 June 1964.
[243] 1961 2 All ER at 453.
[244] *Times*, 28 June 1972.
[245] Hansard, 27 July 1972 col. 1571.
[246] *Times*, 22 June 1972.

Mortimer Q.C.[247] have all formulated versions of such a defence. Here is John Mortimer's:

'Why ever should it be thought fanciful that the defence of public good could apply to advertisements of the sort published in IT? Surely it is at least arguable that it is in everyone's interest that unhappy members of sexual minorities should be in a position to make contact with each other rather than inflict their presumably unwelcome attentions on the community at large. I can conceive of considerable expert medical and psychological evidence which might be called in defence of such advertisements . . .'[248]

Nor is *Knuller* the only case where the prosecuting authorities have acted in breach of the assurance. In 1966 the publishers of 'Black Panther and Pleasure Primer' were convicted of conspiracy to corrupt public morals.[249] And in the prosecution of *Oz*[250] one of the charges was conspiracy to corrupt public morals (in addition to a charge under the Obscene Publications Act); furthermore, the charge was not confined to the advertisements page, but was used to attack the whole magazine. This was a clear breach of the assurance.

But even if the assurance were honoured by the prosecuting authorities publishers would not be guaranteed protection from a charge of conspiring to corrupt public morals – because of the possibility of private prosecutions. This possibility was envisaged by Lord Diplock in *Knuller*:

'Since every private citizen has the right to initiate a prosecution for criminal conspiracy and the executive government has no power to prevent his doing so, it is difficult to see how effect could be given to this assurance except, perhaps, by unprecedented use by the Attorney-General of the power of entering a *nolle prosequi* after the indictment has been drawn; and no steps seem to have been taken to draw the assurance to the attention of the police authorities by whom prosecutions are generally undertaken in the way in which the case was presented to the jury. The instant prosecutions appear to be in breach of it. Yet it seems not improbable that it influenced Parliament in deciding on the contents of the amending Act.'[251]

4. The next objection to the charge of conspiracy to corrupt public morals is that even after *Knuller* the crime remains impossibly vague. This criticism was first voiced by Lord Reid in *Shaw*:

[247] *Times*, 4 July 1972.
[248] *Ibid.*
[249] Hansard H. C. Deb. 26 June 1972.
[250] 1971 3 WLR 939.
[251] 1972 3 WLR at 170–171.

'Finally, I must advert to the consequences of holding that this very general offence exists. It has always been thought to be of primary importance that our law, and particularly our criminal law, should be certain; that a man should be able to know what conduct is and what is not criminal, particularly when heavy penalties are involved. Some suggestion was made that it does not matter if this offence is very wide; no one would ever prosecute and if they did no jury would ever convict if the breach was venial. Indeed, the suggestion goes even further; that the meaning and application of the words "deprave" and "corrupt" (the traditional words in obscene libel now enacted in the Act of 1959) or the words "debauch" and "corrupt" in this indictment ought to be entirely for the jury, so that any conduct of this kind is criminal if in the end a jury think it so. . . . If the trial judge's charge in the present case was right, if a jury is entitled to water down the strong words "deprave", "corrupt" or "debauch" so as merely to mean lead astray morally, then it seems to me that the court has transferred to the jury the whole of its functions as *censor morum*, the law will be whatever any jury may happen to think it ought to be, and this branch of the law will have lost all the certainty which we rightly prize in other branches of our law.'[252]

It has been seen above[253] that the definition of 'corruption' has since been strengthened to mean more than merely lead astray morally; but just how broad the general charge still is may be seen from the attempt to define the offence in chapter 3, and from the words of Lord Reid in *Knuller*, after he had accepted the existence of the offence but was seeking to restrict its application:

'I think that the jury should be told in one way or another that although in the end the question whether matter is corrupting is for them, they should keep in mind the current standards of ordinary decent people.'[254]

But what kind of yardstick is this? Instead of the law being, in Lord Reid's own words, whatever any jury may happen to think it ought to be, the law is now whatever any jury may happen to think that ordinary decent people would think it ought to be.

Lord Diplock's objections to the charge were so strong that he refused to accept that such an open-ended offence could exist at common law:

'*Shaw*'s case upon the count which charged him with conspiring to

[252] 1961 2 All ER 460–461.
[253] page 30.
[254] 1972 3 WLR at 148–9.

corrupt public morals did make it certain that to publish advertisements offering the services of prostitutes was a crime.... The vice of *Shaw*'s case was that it opened a wide field of uncertainty as to what other conduct was also criminal. Previously it was possible for a citizen to regulate his conduct in the knowledge that if what he was minded to do was not specifically prohibited by a criminal statute and did not fall within any of those equally specific categories of conduct which had already been held to constitute offences at common law, he could do it without risk of incurring punishment even though most of his fellow citizens might be shocked at it as immoral or indecent. As a result of *Shaw*'s case it would seem that any conduct of any kind which conflicts with widely held prejudices as to what is immoral or indecent, at any rate if at least two persons are in any way concerned with it, may *ex post facto* be held to have been a crime.'[255]

This is the nub. It is simplistic to talk of the 'current standards of ordinary decent people' as if they were a written code of conduct. For in any modern industrial society there is not one set of standards but many standards; and nowhere more so than in the field of sexual morality where not only the *mores* of different social groups but also the *mores* of different generations differ. Whose morality is to prevail? There is a grave danger that if one moral code is enforced above all others, the adherents of alternative moralities will see in legal decisions merely the prejudice and bias of a certain social group or of a certain generation; and popular respect for the law and its administration by the courts will dangerously diminish.

5. The defenders of the present law maintain that the jury system provides an adequate safeguard. This was emphasized in all the majority speeches in *Shaw*: Lord Morris of Borth-y-Gest's opinion is typical of the prevailing view –

> 'It is said that there is a measure of vagueness in a charge of conspiracy to corrupt public morals, and also that there might be peril of the launching of prosecutions in order to suppress unpopular or unorthodox views. My Lords, I entertain no anxiety on those lines. Even if accepted public standards may to some extent vary from generation to generation, current standards are in the keeping of juries who can be trusted to maintain the corporate good sense of the community and to discern attacks on values that must be preserved.'[256]

[255] 1972 3 WLR at 170.
[256] 1961 2 All ER at 467.

This view was neatly summarized in one sentence by Lord Reid:

> 'In other words, you cannot tell what is criminal except by guessing what view a jury will take, and juries' views may vary and may change with the passing of time.'[257]

And the overwhelming objection to such an extension of the task of the jury has been well expressed by Professor Seaborne Davies:

> 'First, the jury system was never meant to be an alternative for properly enunciated law. Second, it is no more the function of the jury than it is of the judiciary to act as legislators in penal matters.'[258]

The task of the jury in criminal trials should be strictly limited to deciding questions of fact. Once a jury is allowed to stray beyond these limits, it ceases to be an impartial panel and becomes an Inquisition.

6. The final objection to the charge of conspiracy to corrupt public morals lies in the use to which it has been put. A dramatic example of the possibilities inherent in *Shaw* was provided only one week after *Shaw* was finally decided, when the Court of Criminal Appeal heard the case of *R. v. Quinn.*[259] Quinn, better known as Paul Raymond (of Raymond's Revue Bar), was charged with keeping a disorderly house; and at the Old Bailey he was fined £5,000 with 500 guineas costs. The Court of Criminal Appeal upheld this conviction, on the grounds that

> 'a disorderly house is a house conducted contrary to law and good order in that matters are performed or exhibited of such a character that their performance or exhibition in a place of common resort (a) amounts to an outrage of public decency, or (b) tends to corrupt and deprave, or (c) is otherwise calculated to injure the public interest so as to call for condemnation and punishment'.[260]

Ashworth J, giving the judgment of the Court, made it quite clear that this decision (and particularly the category of conduct 'otherwise calculated to injure the public interest') rested heavily on the decision of the House of Lords in *Shaw v. D.P.P.*; and upholding the punishment of Bloom, who was fined £2,500 for the same offence, he said,

> 'in our view the penalty imposed was amply justified, not least as a

[257] *Ibid* at 461.
[258] Presidential Address to the Society of Public Teachers of Law, 1961 6 JSPTL 104.
[259] 1961 3 WLR 611.
[260] *Ibid* at 614.

deterrent to others who may be minded to exploit what is said to be a current craze for strip-tease'.

The details of the offence? '... In some of the scenes actresses appeared either completely nude or practically so. In six and possibly eight out of the seventeen acts constituting the programme matters occurred which far exceeded the limits which the law permits in performances of this sort.' Which *the law* permits? Although this was not a conspiracy case, if instead of 'the law' one reads 'the police backed up by juries and the judges acting as *custodes morum*', then one has an accurate description of how the offence of conspiracy to corrupt public morals is used.

Conspiracy to outrage public decency

This offence may be dealt with much more shortly. The main objections to it are similar to those outlined above: that the charge is impossibly vague, and that it may be put to the most pernicious use. These objections were voiced by Lord Reid in *Knuller*:

> 'I think that the objections to the creation of this generalised offence are similar in character to but even greater than the objections to the generalised offence of conspiracy to corrupt public morals.... To say that published matter offends against public decency adds no new factor; it seems to me to mean no more than that the degree of indecency is such that decent members of the public who read the material will not merely feel shocked or disgusted but will feel outraged. If this charge is an attempt to introduce something new into the criminal law it cannot be saved because it is limited to what a jury might think to be a high degree of indecency.
>
> ... I must now consider what the effect would be if this new generalised crime were held to exist. If there were in any book, new or old, a few pages or even a few sentences which any jury could find to be outrageously indecent, those who took part in its publication and sale would risk conviction. I can see no way of denying to juries the free hand which *Shaw*'s case gives them in cases of conspiracy to corrupt public morals. There would be no defence based on literary, artistic or scientific merit. The undertaking given in Parliament with regard to obscene publications would not apply to this quite different crime. Notoriously many old works, commonly regarded as classics of the highest merit, contain passages which many a juryman might regard as outrageously indecent. It has been generally supposed that the days of Bowdlerising the classics were long past, but the introduction of this new crime might make publishers of such

works think twice. It may be said that no prosecution would ever be brought except in a very bad case. But I have expressed on previous occasions my opinion that a bad law is not defensible on the ground that it will be judiciously administered. To recognise this new crime would go contrary to the whole trend of public policy followed by Parliament in recent times.'[261]

Conspiracy to effect a public mischief

Yet again, in the words of a defender of the two offences, 'virtually all the objections which have been advanced against the offence of conspiracy to corrupt public morals are equally applicable to the offence of conspiracy to effect a public mischief' (Lord Simon of Glaisdale in *Knuller*).[262]

Furthermore, all the objections which have been raised against the substantive offence of committing a public mischief are equally applicable to the conspiracy charge. In *Newland*[263] the Court of Criminal Appeal heaped heavy criticism on the decision in *Manley*,[264] while maintaining on the authorities that such criticism did not apply to the charge of *conspiracy* to effect a public mischief; but on the merits such an argument is entirely specious. Lord Goddard's objections to *Manley* can be applied word for word to the conspiracy charge:

> 'The court is well aware of the caution with which they should approach the consideration of an offence which is alleged to consist of doing acts which tend to effect public mischief as, if extended, it might enable judges to declare new offences which should be the business of the legislature.... No one has ever attempted to define what may or may not constitute a public mischief and we have certainly no desire to increase the number of criminal offences by adding to the category of misdemeanours.... In upholding the conviction [in *Manley*] this court was relying on a dictum of Laurence J. in *Rex. v. Higgins*[265] ... that all offences of a public nature, that is, all such acts as tend to the prejudice of the public are indictable.... It is the breadth of that dictum that was so strongly critised by Sir Fitzjames Stephen in the passage in his History of the Criminal Law to which we have already referred and also by Dr. Stallybrass in the Law Quarterly Review, vol. 49, p. 183. In effect it would leave it to the judges to declare new crimes and enable them to hold anything which they considered to be prejudicial to the community to be a misdemeanour. However beneficial that might have been in days

[261] 1972 3 WLR at 149–150.
[262] 1972 3 WLR at 179.
[263] 1954 1 QB 158.
[264] 1933 1 KB 529, *supra* pages 35–6.
[265] 1801 2 East 5, *supra* page 38.

when Parliament met seldom or at least only at long intervals it surely is now the province of the legislature and not of the judiciary to create new criminal offences ... we believe that the right approach to what may be compendiously called public mischief cases is to regard them as part of the law of conspiracy, and to hold the actions of an individual not committed in combination with others as indictable only if they constitute what has been held in the past to be common law or statutory offences.'[266]

But what is so different about conspiracy? The 'general danger' rationale[267] is no justification for making criminal acts done in combination, when those same acts are lawful if done by an individual. All that the conspiracy charge does in this context is to draw a thin veil over acts of judicial legislation which in *Manley* were performed a little too blatantly. Sayre's criticisms[268] of the Hawkins doctrine[269] could be applied word for word to the charge of conspiracy to effect public mischief:

> 'The truth of the matter is that judges found the Hawkins conception of criminal conspiracy entirely too convenient an instrument for enforcing their own individual notions of justice to be lightly discarded. It enabled judges to punish by criminal process such concerted conduct as seemed to them socially oppressive or undesirable, even though the actual deeds committed constituted of themselves no crime. And in cases where the actual deeds were of doubtful criminality, it saved judges from the embarrassing necessity of having to spell out the crime.'[270]

This last argument applies particularly strongly to the public mischief cases: in all the reported cases, with one or two possible exceptions, the charge was quite unnecessary to obtain a conviction, because the defendant was guilty either of an agreement to commit a crime or of one of the established heads of conspiracy to defraud or conspiracy to pervert the course of justice. The cases are discussed in detail in chapter 3;[271] there is nothing to be gained by going through them again here. Suffice it to say that the analysis of those cases provided above (and with which Smith & Hogan and Glanville Williams, *op. cit.* are in substantial agreement) totally destroys the

[266] 1954 1 QB at 165, 167.
[267] Discussed in chapter 7 below.
[268] 1922 Harv. LR 393.
[269] for which see page 16.
[270] 1922 Harv. LR at 405.
[271] pages 38–43, *supra*.

'floodgates' argument advanced by Lord Hailsham[272] in defence of decisions such as those in *Brailsford*,[273] *Bassey*[274] and *Newland*.[275]

As for the unreported cases,[276] even if some of these cases cannot at the moment be prosecuted except under the charge of conspiracy to effect a public mischief, it does not necessarily follow that the charge should be retained. An alternative solution would be to amend existing legislation or to pass new legislation in order to establish beyond all doubt that the conduct described in those 16 cases is criminal. No one would deny that the anti-social behaviour in those cases *should* be criminal. The question is, who is to declare it so?

> '... [T]he courts have no more power to create new offences than they have to abolish those already established in the law; both tasks are for Parliament' (*per* Lord Simon of Glaisdale in *Knuller*).[277]

The real basis of the public mischief cases is that the charge proved convenient in an age when the scope of statutory and common law offences was not sufficiently comprehensive. They are relics of an earlier stage of legal development which have lost their proper usefulness; their only utility now is for a judiciary which is still anxious to find a justification for judicial legislation. The harm in *Manley*[278] is now dealt with by the Criminal Law Act 1967, section 5(2). The defendants' behaviour in *Leese*[279] is covered by the Race Relations Act 1965. *Shaw* was guilty of offences under the Obscene Publications Act 1959 and the Sexual Offences Act 1956, and the defendants in *Knuller* could have been prosecuted under s.4 of the Sexual Offences Act 1967. And in *de Berenger*, *Brailsford*, *Young* and *Newland* the defendants would either be guilty of conspiracy to defraud or of conspiring to commit the statutory offences of obtaining property or a pecuniary advantage by deception, under the Theft Act 1968, sections 15 and 16.

R. S. Wright made much the same point in relation to conspiracy to effect a public mischief 100 years ago:

> 'In an imperfect system of criminal law the doctrine of criminal agreements for acts not criminal may be of great practical value for the punishment of persons for acts which are not, but which ought to be made punishable irrespectively of agreement.'[280]

[272] Hansard 24 July 1972.
[273] 1905 2 KB 730.
[274] 1931 47 TLR 222.
[275] 1954 1 QB 158.
[276] *supra* pages 43–44.
[277] 1972 3 WLR at 180.
[278] 1933 1 KB 529.
[279] *Times* 19 & 22 September 1936.
[280] *op. cit.* p. 88.

Since then our system of criminal law has lost most of its imperfections; but where there still are gaps of acts which are not, but which ought to be made punishable, it is for Parliament and not for the Courts to fill them in. At a time when Parliament met infrequently and acquiesced in judicial law-making it was in the interests of public order that the courts should determine what conduct ought to be made criminal;[281] but that historical justification has long since disappeared.

[281] See Lord Diplock in *Knuller,* 1972 3 WLR at 164.

5. DEFECTS OF THE PRESENT LAW: PROCEDURE

I. *Roll-up charges of conspiracy*

Conspiracy, unlike attempt, does not sink in the consummated crime. It is thus possible to charge both the substantive crime and a conspiracy to commit it in the same indictment. A roll-up charge is 'the device of charging a defendant with agreeing to do what he did instead of charging him with doing it', which according to Lord Diplock 'has become fashionable in recent years'.[282] Roll-up charges are inserted in indictments by the prosecution because of the substantial procedural advantages which they gain from a trial for conspiracy instead of a trial for the substantive offence. Countless judges have protested against such a practice, but far from diminishing, roll-up conspiracy charges if anything appear to be on the increase.

The injustices which result from such a practice have been dwelt on by several eminent judges. One of the earliest complaints comes from Lord Cranworth L.C. in *Selsby*,[283] and in *Reg. v. Boulton* (1871)[284] Lord Cockburn C.J. said.

> '... when the proof intended to be submitted to a jury is proof of the actual commission of crime, it is not the proper course to charge the parties with conspiracy to commit it, for the course operates, it is manifest, unfairly and unjustly against the parties accused; the prosecutors are thus enabled to combine in one indictment a variety of offences, which, if treated individually as they ought to be, would exclude the possibility of giving evidence against one defendant to the prejudice of others, and which deprive defendants of the advantage of calling their co-defendants as witnesses'.[285]

[282] *Knuller* 1972 3 WLR at 161.
[283] Reported in *Rowlands* 5 Cox CC at 497. Lord Cranworth was then Rolfe B.
[284] 12 Cox CC 87.
[285] *Ibid* at 93.

Lord Cockburn's protest is perhaps slightly exaggerated, since most (but not all)[286] of the evidence admissible on a conspiracy charge will also be admissible on a joint trial for the complete crime. In either case one defendant may be prejudiced by the introduction of evidence which is admissible only against another. The real objection to roll-up charges is that they give 'a semblance of unity to a prosecution which, by combining a number of charges and several defendants, results in a complicated and protracted trial. The jury system is unworkable unless the prosecution is confined to a relatively simple issue which can be disposed of in a relatively short time' (Glanville Williams).[287]

Lord Cockburn's dictum was approved by the Court of Criminal Appeal in *West* (1948),[288] but the warning has had little effect. In *Dawson* (1960),[289] *Davey* (1960)[290] and *Griffiths* (1965)[291] the Court has had to repeat the same warning. In *Dawson*, the first of these three cases, Finnemore J. said:

> 'This court has more than once warned of the dangers of conspiracy counts, especially these long conspiracy counts, which one counsel referred to as a mammoth conspiracy. Several reasons have been given. First of all if there are substantive charges which can be proved, it is in general undesirable to complicate matters and to lengthen matters by adding a charge of conspiracy. Secondly, it can work injustice because it means that evidence, which otherwise would be inadmissible on the substantive charges against certain people, becomes admissible. Thirdly, it adds to the length and complexity of the case so that the trial may easily be wellnigh unworkable and impose a quite intolerable strain both on the court and the jury.'[292]

Dawson was a case involving an indictment of 15 counts and the trial at the Old Bailey lasted 9 weeks. The judgment of the Court of Criminal Appeal was too late to prevent the inclusion of a roll-up conspiracy charge in the indictment in *Davey*, a charge which was the first of 19 counts; the trial lasted 10 weeks. One would have thought that the courts by then would have learnt their lesson; but prosecutors are unusually persistent. In *Griffiths*, five years later, the indictment contained 25 counts and the trial lasted just over 10 weeks. Paull J. in the Court of Criminal Appeal delivered the by now familiar protest:

[286] See below p. 80.
[287] *op. cit.* p. 684.
[288] 1948 1 All ER 718,
[289] 1960 1 All ER 558.
[290] 1960 3 All ER 533.
[291] 1965 2 All ER 448.
[292] 1960 1 All ER at 563.

'From time to time the courts have complained about cases which have proved to be long and complicated because the prosecution have added a charge of conspiracy to substantive counts which would otherwise have been reasonably easy to try on their merits, or alternatively, when it would have been reasonably easy to try the count of conspiracy if taken by itself. . . . We have no hesitation in saying that it was a case where it was almost impossible for any judge to sum up the various issues clearly and at sufficient length without making his summing-up so long as to make it almost certain that the jury would carry no clear picture of all the issues into the jury room. The practice of adding what may be called a rolled up conspiracy charge to a number of counts of substantive offences has become common. We express the very strong hope that this practice will now cease and that the courts will never again have to struggle with this type of case, where it becomes almost impossible to explain to a jury that evidence inadmissible against the accused on the substantive count may be admissible against him on the conspiracy count once he is shown to be a conspirator.... In our judgment, except in simple cases, a conspiracy count (if one is needed at all) should be tried separately to substantive counts.'[293]

Evidence of injustice resulting from the use of roll-up charges is not hard to find. The cases already cited provide three examples. In *West* the Court of Criminal Appeal observed:

'Perhaps there never has been a case in which meticulous care was more clearly called for to ensure that the guilt of any person convicted should be brought home to him by clear evidence directed against himself, and by that only . . . it appears to us probable, in the case of Ellis White and, to a lesser extent, in the case of West, that they were, in fact, hampered in their defence and prejudiced by their inclusion in this vague and general form of charge extending over a period of years.'[294]

In *Dawson* the Court said:

'We think that Wenlock is really a typical example of a man who was sunk by means of a mass of evidence about frauds of various kinds, with the great majority of which he had no connexion either direct or indirect, and in which he took no part whatever. . . .'[295]

And finally in *Griffiths* the same Court said:

'. . . it is now admitted without argument that on two counts on

[293] 1965 2 All ER 449–450.
[294] 1948 1 All ER at 722.
[295] 1960 1 All ER at 563.

which the appellant Bishop was convicted, there was literally no receivable evidence at all against him, the evidence being entries in the appellant Griffiths' books of account, evidence in the conspiracy count once the appellant Bishop is brought into a conspiracy but not evidence on which he can be brought into the conspiracy'.[296]

Why does the prosecution persist in introducing roll-up charges into indictments? Merely to gain procedural advantages at the trial is a very short-sighted aim, since where a roll-up charge goes on appeal the convictions on the conspiracy count are seldom allowed to stand: in *Boulton, West, Dawson, Davey, Griffiths* and *Luberg*[297] the convictions for conspiracy of all the defendants in each case were quashed. The result was that in most of these cases the defendants got away scot free, since the convictions on the other counts were held to be tainted; yet the main defendants could quite easily have been convicted of substantive offences if the prosecution had not insisted on charging them with conspiracy as well – or if the judge had ordered the conspiracy count to be struck out of the indictment.

In recent cases one reason why the prosecution has brought roll-up charges of conspiracy seems to be that this procedure enabled them to bring smaller fish within the net whose presence otherwise would have been totally unjustified. Thus in *Roche and Bowes Egan*[298] Roche was the man who threw the CS gas bomb in the House of Commons, and he was charged with unlawful possession of a firearm; the charge of conspiracy to effect a public mischief seems to have been added merely to try to catch Bowes Egan, a man who was nowhere near the House of Commons at the time and who was eventually acquitted because there was no real evidence against him. Similarly in the first Angry Brigade trial of *Prescott and Purdie*[299] Prescott was charged with two substantive offences in addition to the conspiracy but Purdie was charged only with the conspiracy, there being no direct evidence against him apart from his friendship with Prescott during their time together in Albany prison; Purdie's counsel made a very strong submission at the committal proceedings that there was no case to answer, and at the trial he was acquitted without himself giving any evidence. In the second Angry Brigade trial[300] three out of the four defendants who were acquitted were charged only with conspiracy,[301] but the evidence

[296] 1965 2 All ER at 450.
[297] 1926 19 Cr. App Rep 133.
[298] *Times*, February 18 1971.
[299] *Times*, October-November 1971. Strictly speaking the conspiracy count here was not a roll-up charge: see below, p. 77
[300] *Times*, 7 December 1972.
[301] Bott, McLean and Weir. Christie also faced charges of unlawful possession of firearms. Similar charges against Bott were dismissed by direction of the judge.

alleged against them was rather stronger than that which had been adduced against Purdie.

In the circumstances the conspiracy charge does appear to have been appropriate in the second Angry Brigade trial. All the defendants were charged with conspiracy to cause explosions, but only two (Greenfield and Mendleson) were charged with attempting to cause an explosion; the other counts all related to unlawful possession of firearms, explosives and ammunition. Clearly there was insufficient evidence to prove that any of the defendants had actually caused any specific explosion,[302] but there was sufficient evidence (sufficient anyway for the jury to convict) that four of the defendants had agreed to cause at least some of the explosions. There was *prima facie* evidence of a conspiracy against all the defendants; and the conspiracy charge in this case was *not* a roll-up charge because the substantive offences charged in the other counts of the indictment were not the same offence as was charged in the first count of conspiracy.[303]

A roll-up charge, it should be remembered, is 'the device of charging a defendant with agreeing to do what he did instead of charging him with doing it;'[304] and the test of whether a conspiracy count is a roll-up charge is, Does this count add anything to the indictment? In the Angry Brigade trial the conspiracy count clearly did add something; a simple example of a case where it did not is *Luberg,*[305] where the defendants were charged with conspiracy to defraud and with obtaining and attempting to obtain by false pretences. Here the conspiracy count clearly was a roll-up charge; the defendants were charged with a specific crime and with a conspiracy to commit that crime.[305a] Technically this is legitimate, since conspiracy does not merge in the substantive offence; but judges do have the power to strike such charges out of the indictment on the grounds of duplicity, or they can ask the prosecution to choose one charge only. In the trial of *de Faoit and others*[306] the first count in the indictment, charging a conspiracy to effect a public mischief, was struck out by the judge at the Old Bailey because it did not add anything to the other charges. Such judicial intervention is unfortunately rare, and it has not deterred prosecutors from including a charge of conspiracy to effect a public mischief in a number of recent cases involving explosives (other examples are the Aldershot Bomb trial[307] and the CS gas case[308] in the

[302] Greenfield and Mendleson were found not guilty on the charge connecting them with the bombing of May 22 1970 and October 9 1970.

[303] Apart from counts 2 and 3 against Greenfield and Mendleson; but even there the substantive offences charged related only to two explosions, while the conspiracy was alleged to involve 26.

[304] See note 282.

[305] See note 297.

[305a] But the scope of conspiracy to defraud may be wider than any substantive offence involving fraud: see *infra,* p. 112.

[306] *Guardian* 13 June 1972.

[307] The judge directed a verdict of not guilty on the public mischief count.

[308] *Times,* February 18 1971.

House of Commons). The 'very strong hope' expressed by the Court of Criminal Appeal in *Griffiths* (1965)[309] that the practice of bringing roll-up charges would cease has clearly been disregarded; something stronger than the occasional judicial protest is now called for to control this abuse of conspiracy.

II. *The Rules of Evidence*

Many of the judicial protests cited above have mentioned the loose rules governing the admissibility of evidence as one of the possible injustices of a conspiracy trial. It has sometimes been suggested that special rules of evidence apply to conspiracy cases, but it is probably more correct to say that the rules complained of amount to no more than the special application of two general rules.[310]

The first is the ordinary principle of circumstantial evidence that the existence of any fact may be inferred from the existence of other facts. The agreement of conspirators often has to be inferred in this way, because direct evidence of the agreement is impossible to come by. It is not even essential that all the alleged conspirators should ever have met each other before the trial. It is enough if they each have the same common unlawful purpose.[311]

There are two dangers here. The first is that the importance attached to the acts done may obscure the fact that these acts do not in themselves constitute a conspiracy, but are only evidence of it. The prosecution must prove that the defendants pursued their common unlawful purpose in such a manner that their actions must have been co-ordinated beforehand. This requirement was ignored in *Meyrick*;[312] but it is unlikely to result in any great miscarriage of justice. The second, and far more important, danger is that a defendant may be sucked into a conspiracy of which the only evidence is evidence against the other defendants. This requires a consideration of the second rule, the rule against hearsay.

One of the exceptions to the general rule against hearsay evidence in English law relates to the admissions of agents. The actions or statements of another person are admissible against a defendant, where they are made in his presence or by his authority. When a charge of conspiracy is included in an indictment a form of this exception applies, so that any action or statement by one conspirator and committed in furtherance of the conspiracy is admissible against all the conspirators, whether they were present or had authorized the action or statement or not; *provided* that a foundation for the admission of such evidence is

[309] 1965 2 All ER 448.
[310] See Cross & Wilkins: *Outline of the Law of Evidence*, 3rd Edn. p. 239.
[311] Proved in *Parnell* (1881) 14 Cox C. C. 508 by their membership of the same unlawful society.
[312] (1929) 21 Crim. App. Rep. 94.

laid by independent proof of the conspiracy. This is only a rule of evidence; but its effect is that the defendant in a conspiracy trial has imposed upon him a kind of vicarious liability for the acts and statements of his co-conspirators. Such a rule will clearly operate harshly against defendants whose actual part in the conspiracy has been small; and in practice the requirement that hearsay evidence is only admitted once there is *prima facie* evidence of the existence of the conspiracy is almost impossible to enforce.

The prosecution must prove not only the existence of the conspiracy but also that each defendant was a member of it:

> 'The facts in issue are, whether there was an agreement for the alleged purposes, and whether the defendant was a party to it. Evidence in support of either fact may be given first. . . . If evidence is allowed to be first given of the general matter, that is only provisionally relevant as against a particular defendant, until evidence of the second kind is given. If evidence is first given of the acts of a particular defendant, that is only provisionally relevant as against other defendants. . . .' (R. S. Wright)[313]

The difficulty of course lies in the introduction of evidence on a provisional basis. If independent proof of the conspiracy has not been provided by the end of the trial, then the judge must instruct the jury to disregard the hearsay evidence which has been provisionally admitted. But how can a jury 'forget' inadmissible matter which was nevertheless provisionally admitted and which was highly detrimental to the accused? 'The naive assumption that prejudicial effects can be overcome by instructions to the jury,' Jackson J. has said in the American Supreme Court, 'all practising lawyers know to be unmitigated fiction'.[314] In the same case he had this to say of the hearsay rule in conspiracy:

> 'When the trial starts, the accused feels the full impact of the conspiracy strategy. Strictly, the prosecution should first establish *prima facie* the conspiracy and identify the conspirators, after which evidence of acts and declarations of each in the course of its execution are admissible against all. But the order of proof of so sprawling a charge is difficult for the judge to control. As a practical matter, the defendant is often confronted with a hodge-podge of acts and statements by others which he may never have authorised or intended or even known about, but which help to persuade the jury

[313] *op. cit.* pp. 71–2.
[314] *Krulewitch v. U.S.* (1948) 336 U.S. 440.

of the existence of the conspiracy itself. In other words, a conspiracy often is proved by evidence that is admissible only upon the assumption that the conspiracy existed.'[314]

Glanville Williams[315] has pointed out that the rules of evidence are no different in a joint prosecution for a substantive offence. This is indeed so, but the effect in a conspiracy case is very different, for three reasons:

1. In a conspiracy trial defendants may find themselves in the dock who would never be there in a joint prosecution for a substantive offence: conspiracy spreads its net more widely. Examples are provided by *Roche & Bowes Egan*[316] and *Prescott & Purdie*;[317] there was no substantive offence with which either Bowes Egan or Purdie was, or could have been charged.

2. In a conspiracy trial the test of relevance in order to exclude extraneous evidence is diminished almost to vanishing point. Writing about conspiracy to defraud, Hadden has said,

> 'Neither of the rules of evidence in conspiracy amounts to more than the special application of the general rules of evidence. . . . But their practical effect is to permit the prosecution to bring whatever evidence it has managed to collect on every aspect of the defandant's actitivities.'[318]

In the *Oz* trial[319] the conspiracy charge permitted the prosecution to introduce (presumably prejudicial) evidence of the defendants' life-style – evidence which could hardly have been introduced in a joint prosecution for any substantive offence.

3. In a conspiracy trial the defendant may be charged with conspiring with others unknown, or with others who are known but not in the dock; and once a *prima facie* case of conspiracy is made out and the defendant is shown to be part of it, evidence against those others is evidence against him. A good example is provided by the first Angry Brigade trial, where Prescott was convicted of conspiring with the Stoke Newington Eight, the eight defendants who appeared at the second trial. Much of the evidence against Prescott was drawn from the evidence subsequently produced at the main trial: evidence which Prescott's defence counsel found it difficult to challenge effectively, because the defendants against whom such evidence was primarily

[314] In *Krulewitch v U.S.* (1948) 336 U.S. 440.
[315] *op. cit.* p. 684.
[316] *Times,* February 18 1971.
[317] *Times,* October-November 1971 *passim.*
[318] 1966 CLJ 248.
[319] 1971 3 WLR 939.

admissible were not present. Such evidence could be introduced in a joint prosecution only if all the defendants were prosecuted together.

The effective difference between a joint prosecution and a conspiracy trial may be discerned in this part of the judgment of the Court of Criminal Appeal in *Griffiths*:

> 'It would have been simple ... to have had separate prosecutions against each farmer.... In such a case what was evidence against any farmer would have been simple to resolve. Certainly the appellant Griffiths' books could not be evidence against any of the farmers, none of whom had any knowledge of them. Yet the whole of the appellant Griffiths' method of accounting and whether that method was an honest method or a dishonest method became, in the words of the judge, "the central factor in the case for the prosecution"; a matter hopelessly prejudicial to each and every farmer.'[320]

III. *Presentation of the Defence*

> 'A co-defendant in a conspiracy trial occupies an uneasy seat. There generally will be evidence of wrongdoing by somebody. It is difficult for the individual to make his own case stand on its own merits in the minds of jurors who are ready to believe that birds of a feather are flocked together. If he is silent, he is taken to admit it, and if, as often happens, co-defendants can be prodded into accusing or contradicting each other, they convict each other.' (*Jackson J.* in *Krulewitch v. U.S.*).[321]

Jackson J.'s view of the competence of the jury is probably too pessimistic, but there are undoubted procedural difficulties in the conduct of a conspiracy trial. In the first place, when each defendant has his own counsel, the trial may be greatly lengthened and confused by the repetition of motions and cross-examinations. But it is important that defendants should retain individual counsel, to avoid being associated in the jurors' minds with their co-defendants, and to ensure that where their interests conflict they are adequately protected.

The difficulty for the jury in a long and complex trial lies in remembering the place of each defendant in the alleged conspiratorial pattern, and in determining what evidence applies to which defendants. Something can be done to help them if the judge sums up and takes a verdict for each defendant separately. In *Newland*[322] the Court of Criminal Appeal approved a practice whereby the judge had

[320] 1965 2 All ER at 450–451.
[321] 1948 336 U.S. 440.
[322] 1954 1 QB 158.

charged the jury separately as to each defendant, and had sent the jury out for an individual verdict after each charge. In the second Angry Brigade trial[323] the jury were issued with a kind of score card, with the names of the defendants down one side and a list of the charges against them along the other. Such painstaking efforts to differentiate between the defendants to a conspiracy charge are not always apparent.

IV. *The Drafting of the Indictment*

Because in theory the offence of conspiracy is complete with the agreement the indictment in a conspiracy case need not set out particulars of the overt acts on which the prosecution intends to rely. Thus in an indictment for conspiracy to defraud by false pretences, the false pretences, even when they are known, need not be particularly set out.

In *Patel* (1951)[324] the defendant was charged with fraudulent evasion of tax on a named occasion, and with conspiracy to evade tax; and it was held that evidence could be given on the conspiracy count of evasions on occasions other than that named. Thus the addition of a conspiracy count may enable a defendant to be taken by surprise; it may allow the prosecution to bring 'fishing' charges; and it may keep the judge and jury entirely in the dark as to what exactly the prosecution evidence is meant to establish.

It used to be thought that the judge had power to order particulars of the indictment and that the defendant could apply for such particulars: *Stapleton*.[325] But recent cases have held that a judge is not bound to order particulars, and that the defence can normally glean sufficient information as to the nature of the charge from the depositions, the committal proceedings and prosecuting counsel's opening speech.

The leading case is *Addis*,[326] where the defendant was convicted of conspiracy to defraud such persons as might be induced to part with money to two named companies. He appealed on the ground that the judge should have ordered further and better particulars of the fraud to be supplied. The Court of Criminal Appeal strongly rejected this submission:

> 'The Judge ... was right: there was no obligation on the prosecution to supply any particulars of the count on the indictment, that they did so was merely an act of courtesy; if the particulars in fact given did not help the defence, they could have been ignored.

[323] *Times*, 7 December 1972.
[324] 1951 2 All ER 29.
[325] 1857 8 Cox 69.
[326] 1965 1 WLR 1177n.

Certainly there was no reason why the defence should have been embarrassed. The indictment contained a statement of the offence – conspiracy to defraud. The particulars of the offence were in common form.... All that the defence had to do was to read and digest the depositions and the exhibits and they would have known precisely the case they had to meet.'[327]

In *Williams*,[328] also a case of conspiracy to defraud, the Court of Criminal Appeal laid down that provided the criminal object of the alleged conspiracy is clearly laid, and the conspiracy is one to defraud a named individual, it is not necessary to include in the count any allegation of the specific means which the conspirators are alleged to have agreed should be adopted.

Finally in *Churchill*,[329] a complicated fraud involving over 500 exhibits and 10,000 documents and depositions, one of the defendants applied for an order that the prosecution give the defence particulars in plain English of the overt acts relied upon. His counsel argued that *Addis*[330] had been decided on insufficient argument, and in particular without referring to *Stapleton*[331] and *O'Connell*.[332] Thesiger J., dismissing the application, put the old authorities in their historical context: *O'Connell* had been heard in the days before the Indictable Offences Act 1848, when the defendant only knew the charges that he had to meet from the indictment; and in *Stapleton* there had been no preliminary proceedings, so that apart from the indictment the defendant could only pick up the prosecution case from prosecuting counsel's opening speech. He concluded:

'I can find no case that compels me to hold that the prosecution are bound to plead overt acts in a charge of conspiracy of this nature. On the particular facts of this case, and after hearing the opening, I am not going to exercise any discretion that I have got to order any further particulars....'[333]

It is hard to say in these cases whether the defence applied for further particulars merely as a tactical move, in order to pin the prosecution down to certain alleged overt acts, and so prevent them from relying on other overt acts once the trial had started; or whether the defence genuinely was hampered by not having, as the Indictments Act 1915 requires them to have, 'such particulars as may be necessary for giving reasonable information as to the nature of the charge'.[334] The

327 *Per* Hinchcliffe J. at 1177n–1178n.
328 1964 Crim LR 666.
329 1965 1 WLR 1174.
330 *Supra.*
331 *Supra*
332 1844 11 Cl & F 155.
333 1965 1 WLR at 1181.
334 s. 3(1).

commentator on *Churchill* in the Criminal Law Review certainly thought that the information contained in the exhibits and depositions was insufficient:

> 'Is not the very magnitude of the task when there are 10,000 documents and 500 exhibits a grave embarrassment? And if his Lordship was unable to understand the indictment, how would the jury cope with this as well as with the task of weighing this great mass of evidence?'[335]

(According to this report the judge had said that although he could not understand the indictment, anyone in the trade, such as the defendants, would understand it perfectly well!) And Professor Glanville Williams has argued

> 'that in modern practice particulars of the overt acts should always be required if evidence of them is proposed to be given, and indeed this rule seems to be a fair deduction from the wording of the Indictments Act 1915, s.3(1)'.[336]

While recognizing that in particular cases the defendant may derive sufficient information from other sources, it is submitted that Professor Glanville Williams' proposal should nevertheless be the general rule; particulars of the overt acts relied upon by the prosecution should always be supplied in the indictment.

V. *Evasion of a procedural requirement*

Conspiracy charges may be used by the prosecution instead of a substantive charge in order to evade some statutory safeguard granted by an Act of Parliament. It has already been seen above[337] how the charge of conspiracy to corrupt public morals has been used to deny to the defendant the opportunity to raise the special statutory defence provided by section 4 of the Obscene Publications Act 1959; and how the assurance given to Parliament by the Attorney-General in 1961, that the conspiracy charge would not be so used, is meaningless in the light of its breach in *Knuller* and the possibility of bringing private prosecutions. It is sufficient here to point out the consequences of such an abuse of conspiracy for other statutory safeguards. There is for example a requirement that the leave of the Attorney-General is necessary to bring a prosecution under the Official Secrets Act; technically (and the House of Lords has approved one such technical distinction)[338]

[335] 1965 Crim LR 545.
[336] *op. cit.* at p. 665.
[337] chapter 3, pp. 62–64.
[338] In *Shaw* 1961 2 All ER at 166, commented on by Lord Reid in *Knuller* 1972 3 WLR at 148: see pages 62–63.

this is no bar to a prosecution for conspiracy to infringe the statute itself.

There is however some authority against such a blatant evasion. In *Barnett* (1951)[339] a group of dealers was charged with conspiring to make a bidding agreement. This was a statutory offence which could be prosecuted only with the consent of a Law Officer, and the court very sensibly held that since the alleged conspiracy was substantially the offence created by the Act, the procedure laid down in the Act had to be followed. If the defendants in *Shaw* or *Knuller* had been charged with conspiring to publish an obscene libel, *Barnett* might have been sufficient to stop such a prosecution, quite apart from section 2(4) of the Obscene Publications Act.

[339] 1951 2 KB 425.

6. THE LAW OF PUBLIC ORDER

'It may be true – one has heard it argued both by the House of Lords in its judicial capacity and by textbook writers – that the time has come for Parliament to assume the total mantle of deciding what should and what should not be criminal.... if Parliament assumes that mantle in the light of public discussion, then it will have to put something in the place of the offences which have been created by the law of conspiracy; otherwise there will be a number of wholly unacceptable gaps in the criminal law.' (Lord Hailsham in the House of Lords, 24 July 1972)[340]

One of the spheres of the criminal law in which it is sometimes suggested that there will be a number of 'wholly unacceptable gaps' if conspiracy is removed, or even restricted in its scope, is the law of public order; and the purpose of this chapter is to show that although conspiracy *could* be used extensively to control the activities of demonstrators, squatters, pickets *etc.*, it is not in fact often so used, and indeed there is no need to use it because there are plenty of alternative remedies available. Various aspects of the law of public order will be taken in turn, examining first the role of conspiracy in relation to each, and then what the state of the law would be if conspiracy were removed.

1. *Demonstrations*

The most recent book on the law of public order[341] has this to say of the possible use of conspiracy charges against demonstrators:

'The normal facts of political activity leading to public meetings and demonstrations give wide scope for charges of conspiracy providing the agreement arising prior to the activity has an unlawful object. The object may be the commission of what is in itself a crime and charges may be made of seditious conspiracy.[342] The unlawful object may not be an existing crime but public mischief.... Such charges have not so far been applied to cases involving public order[343] but there is no technical barrier to such application.'

In fact the conspiracy charge has not often been applied to demonstrators. The main reported cases of such a charge being used are

[340] Hansard 24 July 1972 col 1123.
[341] Brownlie: *The Law relating to Public Order* (1968) p. 90.
[342] *Vincent* 1839 9 C & P 91; *O'Connell* 1844 11 Cl & Fin 155; *Lebedoff* (no. 2) 1950 2 WWR 899.
[343] But see *Joshua* 1955 AC 121.

Chandler[344] and *Hain*. In the first six members of the Campaign for Nuclear Disarmament who had helped to organize a demonstration at Wethersfield aerodrome in 1961 were charged with conspiring together and with others to commit a breach of section 1 of the Official Secrets Act 1911 (which makes it an offence to approach or enter any prohibited place for any purpose prejudicial to the safety or interests of the state). The charge in itself was surprising, since the defendants could presumably have been charged with obstructing the highway or obstructing the police in the execution of their duty – or with the substantive offence in section 1 of approaching or entering a prohibited place. What was even more remarkable was that they were not allowed to call any evidence to show that their purpose was not prejudicial to the safety of the state; and that they were given the savage sentence of 18 months' imprisonment.

The facts of *Hain* have already been given.[345] The indictment charged him on the first count with conspiring to 'hinder disrupt interfere with and prevent the exercise of the lawful rights of persons to organize, profit from, play in, watch and otherwise peaceably to enjoy the games of Rugby Football played or arranged to be played during the said tour each of which was a matter of substantial public interest by unlawful means of substantial public concern'; and there were then listed a variety of overt acts in the particulars, some of which were substantive offences[346] and others of which were derived from case-law.[347] The other counts contained similar charges relating to two cricket tours and the 1969 Davis Cup tennis match; and the jury found him not guilty on all counts except that in relation to the tennis match. This perverse verdict (in the light of the much stronger prosecution evidence submitted on the other counts) can only be explained by the jury's dislike of the general conspiracy charge used against him, and their desire to convict him on what appeared to them to be the least serious of the four counts.

It remains to consider whether the conspiracy charges were necessary in these cases, or as a means of controlling demonstrations in general. An American article[348] has suggested that conspiracy charges should be used more frequently in this context, both as a preventive measure (to arrest leaders before the demonstration even takes place) and as a punitive measure to enable the counts to hand down more severe sentences. Fortunately this suggestion has not on the whole been followed in Britain (with the exception of *Chandler*, where the con-

[344] 1962 3 WLR 694.
[345] *Supra*, page 27.
[346] Obstructing the police, watching and besetting under s.7 of the Conspiracy and Protection of Property Act 1875, and causing wilful and malicious damage.
[347] Causing 'harm or annoyance' to players, a test suggested by Lord Halsbury in *Mogul Steamship* 1892 AC 25 (a civil conspiracy case).
[348] 'Mass Demonstrations and Criminal Conspiracies' 1965 16 Hastings L. J. 465.

spiracy charge may have been used to obtain an exemplary sentence); and the reason is that the English criminal law already gives the authorities ample opportunities to control demonstrations.

Many local authorities have powers to prohibit public meetings in parks or public buildings; and the police have the power to stop a meeting if they reasonably believe that disorder is likely to occur. Apart from these administrative weapons, judicial control may be exercised by the power to bind over to keep the peace and be of good behaviour (with sureties if necessary); and by bringing charges of obstructing the police in the execution of their duty (under the Police Act 1964 s.57(3)); using threatening, abusive or insulting words or behaviour (under the Public Order Act 1936 s.5); riot or unlawful assembly; obstructing the highway; and inciting others to commit a nuisance to the public by obstructing the highway.[349] It is not proposed here to discuss the desirability of having all these different offences; what cannot be denied is that the range is extremely wide, and that the prosecuting authorities can cope with every conceivable type of disorder, using minor charges to cope with minor infringements of the peace, and keeping the major charges (*e.g.* riot and unlawful assembly) for more serious disorders.

2. *Sit-Ins*

This is another type of behaviour for which it has been suggested the law does not make adequate provision.[350] The leading case where conspiracy has been charged against students occupying a building is of course *Kamara*; and that is the one case where the civil remedy of an injunction would probably have been inadequate. In the normal sit-in involving the occupation of part of a university or polytechnic, the academic authorities can afford to wait for the brief period necessary to apply for an injunction; but understandably the High Commission in *Kamara* could not.

However there was no need to prosecute the Sierra Leonean students for conspiracy to trespass. In that particular case there was the alternative charge of unlawful assembly and there could also, it is submitted, have been a prosecution under section 7 of the Conspiracy and Protection of Property Act. The section provides that:

> 'Every person who, with a view to compel any other person to abstain from doing or to do any act which such other person has a legal right to do or abstain from doing, wrongfully and without legal authority,

[349] For examples of cases where these charges have been used, see Williams: *The Police, Public Meetings and Public Order* in 1963 Crim LR 149; and for a fuller and more detailed list of possible charges, see Brownlie: *op. cit.*

[350] See *e.g.* letter of Professor Michael Swann, Vice-Chancellor of Edinburgh University, to *Times Education Supplement* (Scottish Edition) February 6 1970.

(1) uses violence to or intimidates such other person or his wife, or children, or injures his property; or
(2) persistently follows such other person about from place to place; or . . .
(4) watches or besets the house or other place where such other person resides, or works or carries on business, or happens to be, or the approach to such house or place; or
(5) follows such other person with two or more other persons in a disorderly manner in or through any street or road;

Shall on conviction . . . be liable either to pay a penalty not exceeding twenty pounds, or to be imprisoned for a term not exceeding three months.'

The Statute was originally passed to establish once and for all that a strike is not a criminal conspiracy; and the subsidiary provisions were designed to limit the action which strikers might take in order to make their strike effective. Section 7 is not however limited to strikers:

> 'It must be borne in mind', Chitty L.J. said in *Lyons v. Wilkins,*[351] 'that the seventh section, although it probably arose out of trade disputes, is not confined to trade disputes or to disputes between masters and men. It applies equally to all Her Majesty's subjects. . . . It would embrace the case of besetting a man's house with a view to compel him not to receive guests or visitors.'

On this interpretation the ambit of the section is very wide indeed; it would appear to make most sit-ins criminal,[352] and certainly covers the sort of behaviour manifested in the Stop the Seventy Tour campaign. Fortunately the prosecuting authorities have shown great reluctance to resort to this Victorian statute, designed for industrial disputes, as a weapon with which to control the activities of today's students; and sit-ins are quite properly regarded as an internal matter for the academic authorities with which the police should not interfere unless they are called in.

3. *Squatters*[353]

The leading case where conspiracy has been used as a charge against squatters is *Bramley*.[354] Bramley and four others conducted a campaign just after the war to house the homeless in empty houses; they were charged *inter alia* with conspiracy to trespass, conspiracy to incite

[351] 1899 1 Ch 255 at 270.
[352] The question is fully researched in Coleman, 'Sit-Ins and the Conspiracy and Protection of Property Act 1875' 1970 Crim LR 608.
[353] See 'Conspiring to Squat' 1971 Crim LR 342.
[354] 1946 11 Journal of Criminal Law 36.

others to commit trespass, conspiracy to commit forcible entry, and with committing forcible entry itself, contrary to the Statutes of Forcible Entry, and they were found guilty on all counts.

The alternative charges in the indictment in *Bramley* provide the key to the way the prosecuting authorities should deal with squatters. Where they enter or detain premises by force they are guilty of effecting a forcibly entry or detainer contrary to the Forcible Entry Acts 1381, 1391 and 1429, and if they are to be prosecuted at all they should be prosecuted for one of these statutory offences. This procedure has been suggested by two different judges in recent possession cases,[355] and their advice was immediately followed in the prosecutions of *Robinson*[356] and *Mountford*.[357] In both these cases the squatters entered peaceably and then proceeded to erect barricades in order to defeat any attempt at eviction. The squatters in *Robinson* thought that the bailiffs would then be guilty of forcible entry, but they did not realise that the later Acts created an offence of forcible detainer, and they were prosecuted for conspiracy to contravene the Act of 1429; they received suspended sentences of 6 months. In *Mountford* the defendant was convicted of the substantive offence of forcible detainer contrary to the 1429 Act and sentenced to 18 months' imprisonment (his defensive preparations included the manufacture of petrol bombs); and at his appeal it was finally established that forcible detainer is an offence in its own right which is triable on indictment.

The primary remedy should however continue to be the landlord's civil action for possession. There is no need to create an offence of conspiracy to trespass; prosecutions should only be brought if the landlord fails to get his possession order enforced, and in those cases a prosecution for forcible detainer will always lie[358] because the squatters must have offered forcible resistance to the landlord's attempt to repossess the property.

4. *Pickets*

The law of conspiracy played a very important (and regrettable) part in industrial disputes in the nineteenth century;[359] but since 1875 strikes and pickets have been given statutory protection. The decision in *Kamara* should not affect most picketing because picket-lines, being outside the factory gates, do not usually involve trespassing on the employer's property; and furthermore peaceful picketing 'in contemplation or furtherance of an industrial dispute' is protected by section 134(1) of the Industrial Relations Act 1971.

[355] *Ex parte The London Diocesan Board of Education* Times Law Report 25 September 1969, and *Re Wykeham Terrace* 1970 3 WLR 649.
[356] 1970 3 WLR 1039.
[357] 1971 2 WLR 1106.
[358] But see Widgery L.J.'s reservations in *Robinson*, 1970 3 WLR at 1044.
[359] See chapter 2.

Where picketing exceeds the limits of the protection provided by the Industrial Relations Act it may be controlled by section 7 of the Conspiracy and Protection of Property Act 1875,[360] which was specifically enacted for that purpose and was used in 1973 in a large number of picketing prosecutions. Typical was the trial in July 1973 at the Mold Crown Court of *Hughes and others,* who were charged with affray and with intimidation under s.7 of the 1875 Act.[360] The particulars of the offence were that they 'together with others not before the Court ... wrongfully and without lawful authority intimidated divers people with a view to compelling those people to abstain from their lawful work'. This trial was the first of five similar cases in the locality and in Shrewsbury at the trial of *Butcher and others*[361] 24 building workers were similarly charged with affray and intimidation under section 7.

But building workers who demonstrated against lump working in Birmingham have been charged with conspiracy to trespass and unlawful assembly[362] – the same charges as in *Kamara.* The prosecution is being brought by the D.P.P. and the defendants include 2 ATV cameramen who were covering the demonstration. The case is not strictly comparable with the others, since it arose out of a demonstration and not out of a picket-line; but it is useful to point the contrast between prosecutions for a statutory offence, which has been created and sanctioned by Parliament, and a prosecution for a common law offence which has recently been created by the courts. As Lord Reid observed in *Shaw v. D.P.P.*, 'Where Parliament fears to tread it is not for the courts to rush in'.[363]

Pickets may also be charged with unlawful assembly, obstructing the highway contrary to s.121 of the Highways Act 1959,[364] and using threatening abusive or insulting words or behaviour, contrary to s.5 of the Public Order Act 1936. There is no need for the conspiracy charge here.

In none of the aspects of the law of public order which we have examined in this chapter does the conspiracy charge add anything to the substantive law. Indeed a recent Report on the Law of Public Order by a Committee of the Society of Conservative Lawyers,[365] which does not once mention the conspiracy charge, concludes:

[360] *supra* pp. 88–89.
[361] *Times* 16 March 1973 (committal), 19 & 20 December 1973 (trial).
[362] *Stevenson & others,* 3–5 December 1973.
[363] 1961 2 All ER at 457.
[364] See *Hunt v Broome,* where the Divisional Court made this an absolute offence; but under s.121 obstruction is only an offence where it is done 'without lawful authority or excuse' – and peaceful picketing within s.134 of the Industrial Relations Act should provide that excuse. The Court held that Broome's picketing although peaceful, had gone beyond s.134 because he had halted a lorry instead of merely speaking to the driver.
[365] Conservative Political Centre, 1970 p. 27.

'The provisions of the law, in the sense of the prescription of offences, are generally adequate in the field of public order.'

The presentation above of the offences covering demonstrations, sit-ins, squatters and pickets has shown that the provisions of the law in this field are more than adequate.

7. THE RATIONALE OF CONSPIRACY

> 'There appear to be great theoretical objections to any general rule that agreement may make punishable that which ought not to be punished in the absence of agreement; for if the act is one which can be done by a person acting alone, and when so done ought not to be punished, it is difficult to see at what point and on what ground criminality can be generally introduced by the fact that two or more persons concur in the act.' (Wright[366])

A certain amount has been written on the rationale of conspiracy in the American literature on the subject,[367] but in England the question has largely been ignored. In America it is traditional to divide the justifications for having a crime of conspiracy into the 'specific object' rationale and the 'general danger' rationale. The former rationale provides a straightforward explanation of conspiracy as an inchoate offence. Conspiracy attacks potentially criminal conduct, but at an earlier stage than attempt; the conspiratorial agreement derives its criminal character purely from the criminal conduct that is the object of the agreement. Under this rationale the agreement is logically punishable only if the conspiratorial objective is a crime.

The 'general danger' rationale is much broader, and provides a justification for punishing not only combinations with criminal objectives but also combinations whose aims are merely considered to be socially undesirable. The argument rests at bottom on the greater threat resulting from the numbers involved in a conspiracy. It was well expressed by the English Criminal Law Commissioners in 1843:

> 'The general principle on which the crime of conspiracy is founded is this, that the confederacy of several persons to effect any injurious object creates such a new and additional power to cause injury as requires criminal restraint; although none would be necessary were the same thing proposed, or even attempted to be done, by any person singly.'

The difference between the two rationales is similar to the distinction between crimes of risk-creation (*e.g.* dangerous driving) and specific crimes of preparation (*e.g.* going equipped for stealing). This is about as far as the two rationales have been developed in the litera-

[366] *op. cit.* p. 86.
[367] See especially 1949 Harv. LR 922, 61 Columb. LR 957, 1970 Yale LJ 872.

ture; it is proposed here to take the analysis of both these concepts a little further, and to reveal them at work in some of the English cases.

1. *The specific object rationale*

As an inchoate offence, like attempt, conspiracy has a preventive function: it legalizes intervention at an earlier stage to prevent a criminal scheme from reaching fruition. Indeed as a prophylactic measure conspiracy is a more effective weapon than attempt because it is not restricted by the requirement of proximity; a criminal conspiracy may exist although the potential social harm is very distant indeed.

The contrast may be brought out by a comparison of the cases of *Rizzo*[368] and *King*.[369] *Rizzo* was an American case in which a gang of armed men who were intending to rob a wages clerk were searching for a victim when they were arrested; and their conviction for attempted robbery was quashed by the New York Court of Appeals on the ground that they had never proceeded beyond the stage of mere preparation. In the English case of *King* the three defendants were seen keeping watch on a wages clerk as he went to the bank, and they were observed consulting together and making notes. When they were arrested a bolt cutter and a length of rubber hose were found in their car. They were charged with conspiracy to rob, and the judge in his summing-up made it clear to the jury that they must be satisfied before they could convict that the defendants had concluded an agreement to rob if the opportunity arose. The defendants were convicted, and their convictions were upheld on appeal.

Such a degree of remoteness from the eventual crime would preclude the punishment of a single would-be criminal; so that numbers enter even into the specific object rationale – the justification for intervention at such an early stage is that the crime is more likely to be committed if there is more than one person involved. Numbers are felt to increase the criminal risk because it will be harder for the individual defendant to stop the wheels he has set in motion; the moral support of the group strengthens the determination of each member, and the numbers in the group make for greater efficiency through division of labour, and enable it to realize more ambitious crimes. This anyway is the theory; but in some cases a large number of criminals might increase the risk that the plan will be leaked, and a sharing of uncertainties might lead the defendants to be more easily dissuaded. At the very least, it would seem reasonable that as the agreement gets further and further away from the contemplated crime, lessening the probability that it will ever occur, the justification for punishing the agreement must likewise decrease – there must be a serious threat of social harm before the intervention of the criminal law can be justified. But numbers enter the

[368] 1927 246 N.Y. 334.
[369] 1966 Crim LR 280.

specific object rationale only in a very limited way: they merely justify intervention in what is already a criminal scheme (*i.e.* one with a criminal object) at an earlier stage – they do not justify making criminal a plan whose objective is merely immoral or socially injurious.

2. *The Rationale of Conspiracy in England – Some Cases Examined*

In certain cases agreements have been punished where the criminal objective was incapable of fulfilment: an example is *Whitchurch*,[370] a conspiracy to abort a woman who was not pregnant. Here the justification of punishment must be risk-creation, *i.e.* the general danger rationale: the defendant, although incapable of committing this particular offence on this particular occasion, has manifested his desire to do the kind of harm proscribed by law.[371] But English law does not always take this attitude. In *B.o.T., v. Owen*[372] the House of Lords held that an agreement made in England to commit an act that was unlawful only in Germany (it involved defrauding a German export control department) was not an indictable cospiracy.[373] This decision clearly relies on the specific object rationale: under the general danger rationale a conviction would have been justified – a group within the jurisdiction which feels itself at liberty to choose whether or not to obey the law of a foreign country presents a social danger which needs to be curbed. This was in fact an idea the House of Lords toyed with: their Lordships reserved the question 'whether a conspiracy in this country which is to be wholly carried out abroad may not be indictable here on proof that its performance would produce a public mischief in this country. . . .'

Throughout the conspiracy cases English law hesitates uncertainly between the two rationales. Examples where the general danger rationale is uppermost are to be found in some of the differences between the rules for attempt and conspiracy, and in the rule in *Verrier v. D.P.P.*[374] that a heavier punishment can be imposed for conspiracy than could be imposed for the completed crime. The first of the different rules for attempt and conspiracy is that it cannot be a criminal offence to attempt to do something which is not an offence; but with conspiracy it can (*e.g.* conspiracy to trespass). Nor can a person attempt to commit a summary offence;[375] but a conspiracy to commit a summary offence is an indictable offence. Similarly with the rules of merger – attempt sinks in the consummated crime,[375a] but conspiracy does not; so that it is pos-

[370] 1890 24 QBD 420.

[371] Such a policy justification is not confined to the crime of conspiracy: see *e.g.*, the case of *Ring* (1892) 17 Cox 491, where a man was convicted for attempting to steal from an empty pocket.

[372] 1957 AC 602.

[373] Lord Tucker said: 'No one has ever been convicted of such a conspiracy and if it is in the public interest that such conspiracies should be triable and punishable here, it is, I think, for the legislature so to determine' – a marked contrast with the confidence of the House of Lords in *Shaw*.

[374] 1967 2 AC 195.

[375] This is merely the better view: there is no authority directly in point.

[375a] *Males* 1962 2 QB 500, and *Rogers v. Arnott* 1960 2 QB 244. But see now Criminal Law Act 1967 s.6(4) as a result of which the doctrine of merger only applies (if it still applies at all) to summary trial: see Smith & Hogan, 3rd Edn., p. 206.

sible to charge both the substantive crime and a conspiracy to commit it in the same indictment. The justification offered for all these anomalies is the general danger argument that the combination to do an unlawful act may be more dangerous than the actual doing of that act. This seems nonsensical, if the conspiracy is held to be criminal because its object is a crime; because then the measure of its danger can only be the risk of such a culmination. But the general danger rationale holds that the criminality of a conspiracy lies in *more* than merely the criminal objective. But of what does this 'more' consist? What other test of social danger can be applied?

Similar arguments apply to the decision in *Verrier v. D.P.P.*[376] Verrier was convicted on an indictment containing one count only, of conspiracy to defraud; and he was sentenced to seven years imprisonment. The maximum statutory punishment at the time, on one charge of obtaining money by false pretences, was five years; and since Verrier had only planned to commit one offence (a fraudulent claim for life insurance by making the policy-holder 'disappear') he appealed against sentence. The House of Lords held that it would be wrong to give a greater sentence for attempt than could be given for the substantive offence; but upheld a greater sentence for conspiracy 'if it had been commtted where the circumstances warranted, as here, the conclusion that the conspiracy was a crime different from and more serious than the substantive offence'.

The House of Lords also approved a passage from Wright:

> 'There may be cases in which the agreement or concurrence of several persons in the execution of a criminal design is a proper ground for aggravation of their punishment beyond what would be proper in the case of a sole defendant. Such would be cases in which the co-operation of several persons at different places is likely to facilitate the execution or the concealment of a crime, or in which the presence of several persons together is intended to increase the means of force or to create terror, or cases of fraud in which suspicion and ordinary caution are likely to be disarmed by the increased credibility of a representation made by several persons.'[377]

But Wright merely says that such considerations justify the aggravation of punishment 'beyond what would be proper in the case of a sole defendant'; he does not say that they justify increasing the punishment beyond the maximum set by Parliament. The House of Lords held that this was 'not an improper exercise of their judicial discretion'; and the argument here is not really about what test of social danger is to be

[376] *supra.*
[377] *op. cit.* pp. 81–82.

applied, but *who* is to apply it. And surely the answer must be that Parliament, having set a statutory maximum for a type of offence, is the only body competent to decree the exceptions to that maximum.

A similar decision to *Verrier v. D.P.P.* is that in *Blamires Transport Services*[378] where a group of lorry drivers who combined to exceed their statutorily permitted hours (a summary offence) were punished with more than the maximum for that offence. Of such decisions Wright said:

> 'But on the whole it is conceived that there can be very few kinds of minor offences, the quality of which can be so altered by agreement as to make it necessary to punish them by indictment; and that these kinds ought to be considered beforehand by the legislature and specified in the written law.'[379]

Precisely these considerations apply here. Where the nature of an offence is so altered by its being committed in combination that a punishment greater than the statutory maximum is called for, Parliament and Parliament alone must provide for this. Otherwise defendants will suffer penalties greater than they could have anticipated when they started on their course of criminal conduct.

3. *The general danger rationale*

The general danger rationale may in part have crept in from the law of civil conspiracy. How easily the courts tend to run the tort and the crime together may be seen from this definition given by Lord Brampton in *Quinn v. Leathem*:

> 'A conspiracy consists of an unlawful combination of two or more persons to do that which is contrary to law, or to do that which is wrongful and harmful towards another person. It may be punished criminally by indictment, or civilly by an action on the case. . . .'[380]

Such a close association inevitably gives rise to much slipshod thinking, as the American Jackson J. has pointed out:

> 'The interchangeable use of conspiracy doctrine in civil as well as penal proceedings opens it to the danger, absent in the case of many crimes, that a court having in mind only the civil sanctions will approve lax practices which later are imported into criminal proceedings.'[381]

[378] 1964 1 QB 278.
[379] *op. cit.* p. 85.
[380] 1901 AC 495 at 528.
[381] *Krulewitch v U.S.* 1948 336 US 440.

And indeed it is not hard to find formulations of the general danger rationale in the civil cases, for example Lord Macnaghten in *Quinn v. Leathem*:

> '... a conspiracy to injure might give rise to civil liability even though the end were brought about by conduct and acts which by themselves and apart from the element of combination or concerted action could not be regarded as a legal wrong.'[382]

The basis of the general danger rationale is that numbers pose a greater social danger:

> 'though you may assert your rights against one individual, how can you defend your rights against a number of persons combined together to inflict a wrong on you?'[383]

This Numbers Argument suffers from two main weaknesses. In the first place, as a generalization it is much too simplistic. A single man blowing a whistle on the streets at night might constitute no nuisance; and 100 men doing the same in combination might well be committing a public nuisance; but how is it that precisely the same effect, which is perfectly lawful when produced by *one,* becomes criminal when produced by *two*? Conspiracy is not like riot, which can only be committed by three or more persons, because it is impossible for one man alone to produce the anti-social effects known as a riot, while it is quite possible with many crimes for a single defendant to cause exactly the same effects as a combination.

The second weakness of the general danger rationale is that the *mens rea* of two men committing an offence in combination will not usually be any different from that of a single offender. On retributive grounds at least there can be no reason for punishing the two men more severely than the single man; and certainly there can be no retributive reason for punishing two men for conduct which if done by one man would not be punishable. The punishment then can only be justified on grounds of public policy; and at its most plausible the public policy argument can sometimes be quite convincing. In *Parnell*,[384] a case rather similar (on its legal facts) to *Kamara*, a group of Irishmen were charged *inter alia* with conspiring to incite a rent strike. Defence counsel argued, as in *Kamara*, that 'there could be no indictable conspiracy unless the thing to be done or the means by which the thing

[382] 1901 AC 495 at 510, adapting the words of Lord Watson in *Allen v Flood* 1898 AC 1 at 108.
[383] Fitzgerald J. in *Parnell* 1881 14 Cox 508 at 514.
[384] 1881 14 Cox 508.

was to be done were in themselves criminal';[385] but this argument was vigorously denied by the court:

> 'If it be asked on what principle a combination of several to effect ... [a] ... wrongful purpose becomes an offence, the answer is, upon the same principle that any other civil wrong, when it assumes a more aggravated and formidable character, is constituted an offence, and becomes transferred from the domain of the civil to that of the criminal law. All offences ... are either in their nature offences against the community, or are primarily offences against individuals. As regards the latter case, every offence against person or property, or other individual right involves a civil wrong, which would have entitled the person injured to civil redress were it not that owing to the aggravated nature of the wrong and the general insecurity to society which would ensue from such acts, if allowed to go unpunished, the State steps in, and merging the wrong done to the party immediately interested in the larger wrong done to the community, converts the wrong done by the infraction of the individual right into a crime, and subjects the wrong doer to punishment to prevent as far as possible the recurrence of the offence. Thus the dividing line between private wrongs, as entitling the party injured to civil remedies, and private wrongs thus converted into public wrongs, in other words into offences and crimes, is to be found in the more aggravated and formidable character which the violation of individual rights under given circumstances assumes. It is upon this principle that the law of conspiracy, by which the violation of private right, which if done by one, would only be the subject of civil remedy, when done by several is constituted a crime, can be vindicated as necessary and just.'[386]

It is interesting to compare this argument with the test proposed by Stable J. in *Bramley*:[387]

> 'If ... having regard to the scope of the combination ... and to the numbers involved, and the methods adopted ... this matter resolves itself into something which transcends that sphere where the property owner aggrieved can go to the civil court ... and passes into that sphere where it becomes a matter of public concern ...' *etc.*

In both cases the argument is attractive and full of common sense; the only difficulty is *who* is to decide when a wrong to an individual

[385] *ibid* at 519.
[386] *per* Barry J. at p. 520.
[387] 1946 Journal of Criminal Law 36; *supra* p. 56.

becomes an offence against society? 'The judge? The jury? Are either competent? . . . If the judge is to decide, he may well take the verdict from the jury; if the jury is to decide, part of the law of conspiracy can be stated in four words: "*salus populi, suprema lex*".'[388] This is the fundamental objection to the general danger rationale. Neither judge nor jury is competent to draw the line between what is the concern of the criminal law and what is not; that is a legislative function which must be left to Parliament. Yet the general danger rationale has been used to justify imposing a sentence above the maximum allowed by Parliament for the substantive offence; and it has been used to justify making criminal acts done in combination when those same acts done by an individual would not be a crime.

The general danger rationale inevitably involves a degree of judicial legislation which today is unacceptable, and it is time that it was abandoned. It is logically unsound and in its implementation extremely dangerous. The proposals in chapter 9 below follow as a logical consequence of restricting the rationale of conspiracy to its function as an inchoate offence. In Wright's words,

> 'A law which directs the prosecution or punishment . . . of an agreement for a crime is merely auxiliary to the law which creates the crime'.[389]

If the general danger rationale is rejected it follows that conspiracy must be limited to agreements to commit crimes; that the rules in the law of attempt relating to merger and to summary offences should apply to conspiracy, at least to the extent that a conspiracy to commit a summary offence should not be more than a summary offence; and that a punishment for conspiracy should not exceed the statutory maximum for the substantive offence. These in summary are some of the reforms proposed in chapter 9.

[388] Lawton L.J. in *Kamara*, 1972 3 All ER at 1005.
[389] *op. cit.* p. 80.

8. CONSPIRACY IN OTHER LEGAL SYSTEMS

'Attribution of criminality to a confederation which contemplates no act that would be criminal if carried out by any one of the conspirators is a practice peculiar to Anglo-American law. . . . The doctrine does not commend itself to jurists of civil law countries, despite universal recognition that an organised society must have legal weopans for combatting organised criminality. Most other countries have devised what they consider more discriminating principles upon which to prosecute criminal gangs, secret associations and subversive syndicates.' (Jackson J. in *Krulewitch v. U.S.*)[390]

a) *Civil Law countries*[391]

It is important right at the outset to enter a caveat as to the limitations of what can be learnt from a study of foreign systems. The common law concept of conspiracy is unknown in most European countries; but it would be rash to deduce from that fact alone that we would do better without it. European systems may be able to manage without a crime of conspiracy because their penal codes provide them with alternative safeguards; and only a detailed study of the criminal law of each country would reveal this. Here we must be content with a comparison of the broad principles.

In general the concept of conspiracy as something punishable even where no crime has been committed is unknown in civil law systems. Conspiracy is regarded not as an inchoate offence but as a crime of criminal organization. Concerted action is a basis for aggravating penalties; and certain exceptional conspiracies may be prosecuted at an inchoate stage – primarily those directed against the security of the state.

The Italian Penal Code of 1930 is perhaps the best expression of the civil law approach. Article 115, para. 1 reads:

'Except where the law provides otherwise, whenever two or more persons agree for the purpose of committing an offence, and it is not committed, none of them is punishable for the sole fact of making an agreement.'

The judge may however apply a 'police measure' (liberty under supervision) to the defendants. The most important exceptions to this general rule are crimes against the international and internal personality of the state (Articles 302–7) – the equivalent to the English offences of treason and sedition. Apart from these essentially political offences

[390] 1948 336 US 440.
[391] For a useful survey see Wagner: Conspiracy in Civil Law countries 42 J.C.L.C.P.S. 171.

conspiracy is only an offence if three or more persons join together to commit more than one crime (Article 416, an anti-Mafia measure).

In France Article 265 of the Code Penal, which is entitled Association de Malfaiteurs, makes criminal 'Every group, however small or short-lived, or agreement which has as its object the organization or commission of *crimes* against persons or property'. This seems to be nearer to the English offence of conspiracy, but the word *crimes* has a special meaning which significantly limits the scope of the Article.[392] In the first place, the plural is intentional: the agreement, as in Italy, must be to commit more than one crime. Secondly, *crimes* (as opposed to *infractions correctionnelles*, *i.e.* misdemeanours) include only very serious offences, such as aggravated theft, aggravated assault, forging money, or crimes against the security of the state. Certain other offences (rape, theft, indecent assault, procuring, sedition and vagrancy) when committed in combination may be more severely punished; but the combination itself is not indictable when the crime is not committed.

The principles of German law are essentially the same. In the Code of 1871 conspiracy was only a crime for offences against the state; now Article 4 provides that conspiracy includes an agreement to commit a 'major crime'.

b) *Common Law Systems*

1. *The English Draft Code of 1879*

It is often forgotten that an early attempt to codify English criminal law was made by the Royal Commission appointed to consider the law relating to Indictable Offences, which reported in 1879. Conspiracy is classified in Part XXXVI of their Code along with threats and attempts and incitement, and it is limited in ss. 419 and 420 to agreements to commit indictable offences. Other conspiracies which are specifically made criminal by the Code are agreements to bring false accusations, to pervert the course of justice, to defile women, to defraud, and to prevent by force the collection of rates and taxes. All other agreements would have been lawful.

II. *American Law*

The American common law is similar to that in England, and has given rise to similar protests, both academic[393] and judicial.[394] What is of interest in America are the different attempts to codify the law – the Federal Statutes, the various State Codes, and the Model Penal

[392] See the commentary in Juris-Classeur Penal 11 1964, page 7.
[393] *e.g.* Sayre 1922 Harv LR 393.
[394] See especially Jackson J. in *Krulewitch v US, supra*; and in *Dennis v US* (1957), where he described conspiracy as "a dragnet device capable of perversion into an instrument of injustice".

Code produced by the American Law Institute. Many of the States have limited conspiracy to combinations to commit crimes; others have retained the criminality of agreements to commit a wide range of unlawful acts. An example is the Utah Code, which makes criminal conspiracy 'to commit any act injurious to the public morals, or to trade or commerce, or for the perversion or obstruction of justice. . . .' In *Musser v. Utah* (1947)[395] the defendants appealed against a conviction under this section on the grounds that the law was so uncertain that it violated the constitutional principle of due process. The US Supreme Court remanded the case for determination whether the statutory language was sufficiently defined to afford a reasonable standard; but at the same time it made its own views quite clear:

> 'Standing by itself, it would seem to be warrant for conviction for agreement to do almost any act which a judge and jury might find at the moment contrary to his or its notions of what was good for health, morals, trade, commerce, justice or order.'[396]

But the most interesting of all the American Codes is the Model Penal Code.[397] The Code limits conspiracy to agreements to commit crimes; and the Final Draft (1970) gives this definition:

> 's. 5.03(1) *Definition of Conspiracy*. A person is guilty of conspiracy with another person or persons to commit a crime if with the purpose of promoting or facilitating its commission he:
> a) agrees with such other person or persons that they or one or more of them will engage in conduct which constitutes such crime or an attempt or solicitation to commit such crime; or
> b) agrees to aid such other person or persons in the planning or commission of such crime or of an attempt or solicitation to commit such crime'.[398]

The authors of the Code rejected the third head of conspiracy (to commit a public mischief or to corrupt public morals), and also conspiracy to defraud and conspiracy to pervert the course of justice, because 'such provisions fail to prove a sufficiently definite standard of conduct to have any place in a penal code'. They went on to say:

> 'We acknowledge that there are some activities that should be criminal only if engaged in by a group, but we believe they should be dealt with by special conspiracy provisions in the legislation governing the general class of conduct in question, and they should be no

[395] 333 US 95.
[396] 333 US 95 at 97.
[397] The authors of the sections on attempt and conspiracy have provided a very useful explanation in 'The Treatment of Inchoate Crimes in the Model Penal Code' 1961 Columb. LR 571 and 957.
[398] All quotations from the Code are to be found in 1961 Columb. LR 957 *et seq.*

less precise than penal provisions generally in defining the conduct they proscribe.'[399]

It is worth noticing also that the Code's definition of conspiracy is 'unilateral': attention is directed to each individual defendant's culpability by framing the definition in terms of the conduct which suffices to establish the liability of any given defendant, rather than the conduct of the group. On the English definition of conspiracy as an 'agreement between two or more persons', if only one defendant is charged or if two are charged but one is acquitted, then the charge must be dismissed because of the impossibility of one person forming a conspiracy with himself. The unilateral approach by focusing on the individual's culpability avoids those 'technical' problems which arise when the second conspirator is not prosecuted, or when he has feigned the agreement.[400]

The third respect in which the Model Penal Code's definition is a great improvement over the English law of conspiracy is in its specification of the degree of *mens rea* required. The traditional formula says nothing about the defendant's state of mind except insofar as the concept of agreement itself carries certain implications about his attitude towards the crime. S. 503 (1) provides more precise standards. It requires in all cases a 'purpose to promote or facilitate' the commission of the crime; and in addition it requires that the defendant agrees either (a) that he or one or more of the others will commit the crime, or (b) that he will aid in the planning or commission of the crime. This requirement of purpose resolves the problems which arise when a defendant is charged whose relationship to a criminal plan is essentially peripheral; an example would be a man who sells sugar to a group of illegal distillers, or a defendant who is no more than the messenger-boy for a gang planting bombs.

The Code also provides a neat solution to determine the limits of 'wheel' and 'chain' conspiracies:

> 's. 5.03(2). *Scope of the conspiratorial relationship.* If a person guilty of conspiracy . . . knows that a person with whom he conspires to commit a crime has conspired with another person or persons to commit the same crime, he is guilty of conspiring with such other person or persons, whether or not he knows their identity, to commit such crime.'

And finally the Code provides for a right of severance where a

[399] *ibid.* p. 965.
[400] This second problem has never come before an English court; but see the decision of the Canadian Supreme Court in *R v O'Brien* 1955 2 DLR 311 which held that there could be no agreement where one party did not intend to carry out the unlawful purpose.

defendant requests this and the court deems it necessary to the fair determination of his guilt or innocence (s.5.03(4)). This right also exists at English law, but it is rarely granted because of the obvious convenience of a joint trial which allows the prosecution to present at one trial all aspects of an entire scheme. In large-scale frauds or long and complex trials such as that of the Angry Brigade such a scheme of presentation may be essential (indeed we have argued above[401] that Prescott's separate trial may have worked injustice on him).

III. *Commonwealth jurisdictions*

Australian law has the same common law definition of conspiracy as English law; and some of the State Codes (*e.g.* Queensland) have even reproduced the Denman formula word for word. In Canada the Denman formula is also part of the Criminal Code; but in Canada[402] as in Australia[403] academic lawyers have been anxious to exclude the authority of *Shaw v. D.P.P.* In New Zealand and in South Africa conspiracy is restricted to agreements to commit crimes.

[401] pages 80–81.
[402] See 23 Toronto Faculty of Law R. 129.
[403] See Howard: *Australian Criminal Law* (1965).

9. PROPOSALS FOR REFORM: THE SUBSTANTIVE LAW

'Consequently the law ought to be changed so that only agreements to commit fairly serious crimes could form the subject matter of indictable conspiracies. The burden, then, must fall on those who wish to make out a case for bringing other specific matters within the law to propose particular statutory provisions as they find them necessary.' (Baroness Birk)[404]

The Case for Legislation

No significant reform of the law of conspiracy can now be achieved except by legislation. It has sometimes been suggested that the decision of the House of Lords in *Bhagwan*, and its abandonment in *Knuller* of its self-appointed role as *custos morum*, are indications that the courts themselves may be expected to reform the law; but any such belief is pure delusion. Those who put their faith in the arguments of Lord Diplock and Lord Reid as the catalysts of reform ignore the fact that in *Knuller* and in *Shaw* those arguments were voted down in a 4:1 defeat; and they also ignore the fact that in certain quarters the recent judicial retreat has not even been recognized. Thus Lord Hailsham, speaking in the House of Lords after the judgment in *Knuller,* said quite blandly:

'Of course it is true that the majority of the House of Lords in both cases [*Knuller* and *Shaw*] decided that there was a residual right of the criminal courts of this country to extend the boundaries of conspiracy in an unidentifiable number of cases.'[405]

But most important of all, the courts themselves have said time and time again that it is too late now to alter the law except by legislation.

There is no lack of examples. Lord Morris of Borth-y-Gest, a supporter of the present law, stated the position robustly in *Knuller*:

'It was clearly held in *Shaw*'s case that there had been and that there continued to be as part of the criminal law of England the offence of conspiracy to corrupt public morals. . . . There are some who regret that there should be such an offence and who would wish

[404] Hansard 24 July 1972.
[405] Hansard 24 July 1972.

to change the law: their course is to persuade Parliament to change it. Once this House in its judicial capacity was satisfied that the offence was known to and existed as part of the law it would neither have been proper nor would it have been within its judicial province to proclaim or to suggest that the law should be forgotten or ignored or that its force should be denied.'[406]

Lord Reid, regretfully joining the majority in *Knuller,* put the position more succinctly:

'I said in *Shaw*'s case and I repeat that Parliament and Parliament alone is the proper authority to change the law with regard to the punishment of immoral acts. Rightly or wrongly the law was determined by the decision in *Shaw*. Any alteration of the law as so determined must in my view be left to Parliament.'[407]

Nor is this judicial abdication of responsibility confined to the offence of conspiracy to corrupt public morals. In *Kamara* we find the Court of Appeal saying, in mixed tones of defiance and despair:

'Whatever private views we may have about the desirability at the present time of having a definition of a crime in such wide terms, we feel bound to declare that the law is as stated by Willes J. in *Mulcahy*'s case; ... it must follow that an agreement to trespass is an indictable conspiracy, no matter what absurd results can be envisaged. . . .'[408]

And in the House of Lords Lord Hailsham, while narrowing down the scope of conspiracy to trespass, indicated the limits of what can be achieved by the courts because of the constraints of precedent:

'In my opinion, it is now far too late without legislation to establish, even were it otherwise desirable, that indictable conspiracy is limited to cases where the illegal elements in the action contemplated would be punishable as a crime if committed by a single individual. I base this view partly on the history of the matter, and partly on a multiplicity of judicial dicta and decisions to this effect.'[409]

Finally, the whole history of the common law development of conspiracy has shown a steady expansion of the scope of the offence. The

[406] 1972 3 WLR at 154.
[407] 1972 3 WLR at 147.
[408] 1972 3 All ER at 1004 and 1005.
[409] 1973 3 WLR 198 at 208.

only occasion when the growth of a branch of conspiracy has been halted was when Parliament intervened in the nineteenth century to undo the bitter legacy[410] left by the courts' use of the conspiracy weapon against the trade unions. Now it is time that Parliament intervened again.

The Substantive Law

At the beginning of this book it was said that the complete abolition of conspiracy was beyond the scope of this enquiry; but in the light of the evidence (admittedly slender) from civil law systems, and the very grave procedural disadvantages facing the defendant in conspiracy trials, complete abolition does deserve consideration at least as a *conceptual* possibility. For a reform of the substantive law which reduces conspiracy to agreements to commit crimes, while cutting out some of the worst abuses of conspiracy will not do anything to solve the *procedural* difficulties; and if the procedural difficulties are considered insurmountable[477] then abolition should be considered as one possible solution.

Such a change would of course involve a major re-drawing of the boundaries of criminal responsibility in English law; but to some extent what is lost by abolishing conspiracy can be gained by extending the scope of attempt backwards, so that the law can intervene at an earlier stage than that at present permitted by the requirement in attempt of a 'proximate act'. A reform of this kind would do away with the present anomaly that one man performing mere 'acts of preparation' as they are understood in the law of attempt cannot be convicted of a criminal offence, while two men performing those same acts in concert can be convicted of conspiracy (such an anomaly can only be justified by a version of the Numbers Argument in the 'general danger' rationale described in chapter 7).

It would of course be extremely difficult – perhaps impossible – to define satisfactorily the new stage where liability for a criminal scheme of preparation begins. But the 'proximate act' requirement is a notoriously difficult boundary anyway, so that the change would probably involve only a shifting of our difficulties rather than an aggravation of them. In doing this it is almost certainly preferable to try to evolve some general formula for determining the moment when criminal liability falls, rather than trying to extend attempt backwards by legislating that half a dozen or a dozen specified acts of preparation will henceforth constitute proximate acts, as the Model Penal Code does.[412]

Further development of this line of enquiry is unfortunately impossible here, because it involves a much deeper analysis of the other

[410] The words are those of Lord Diplock in *Knuller*, 1972 3 WLR at 168: see chapter 2.
[411] Some proposals for procedural reform are discussed below, pp. 119–123.
[412] See 1961 Columb. LR 571.

inchoate offences of incitement and attempt, and the discussion should really be carried out within the framework of specific cases.[413] For the moment it is assumed that conspiracy will be retained in some form, and discussion is limited to what that form should be.

There can be no doubt that the present scope of conspiracy should be severely restricted. This is the unavoidable conclusion which flows from all the evidence presented in the foregoing pages. Analytically the simplest reform would be to restrict conspiracy to agreements to commit a crime, and so reduce it to its proper role as an inchoate offence on a par with incitement and attempt. This was the proposal presented by Baroness Birk to the House of Lords in her amendment to the 1972 Criminal Justice Bill:

> 'Amendment 36A, Abolition of Common Law Conspiracy.
> 1) Notwithstanding any rule of law or practice to the contrary no offence shall be committed by any person in agreeing or conspiring with another or others to do or not to do anything whatsoever unless:
>   a) it is an offence by virtue of any enactment or at common law to do or not to do that thing
>   b) it is an offence by virtue of any enactment so to agree or conspire.'[414]

Amendment 37(1) limited conspiracy to agreements to commit indictable offences, which was the recommendation of the 1879 Draft Code, and which would bring conspiracy into line with the rule for attempt. Amendment 37(2) provided that the maximum punishment for conspiracy should not exceed the maximum that could be passed for the full offence (thus abolishing the rule in *Verrier v. D.P.P.*).[415] And finally Amendment 38 enacted that effecting a public mischief and corrupting public morals were not in themselves offences at common law; for if these were substantive offences then a conspiracy to commit them would be indictable as a conspiracy to commit a crime.

The effect of Baroness Birk's proposals would be to eliminate the second and third heads of conspiracy, and to limit the first head to agreements to commit indictable offences. While no tears need be shed at the abolition of the third head, there are certain objections to the other two proposals which deserve to be taken seriously. The first two objections were raised by Lord Widgery:

1) 'I take up your Lordships' time for only a moment or two to deal with one or two of the cases where I suggest real merit remains.

[413] E.g. *Rizzo* 1927 246 NY 334 and *King* 1966 Crim LR 280, discussed in chapter 7. p. 94.
[414] Hansard 24 July 1972 Col 1104.
[415] 1967 2 AC 195: see chapter 7.

The first is the existence of conspiracy to commit a summary offence, which under this Amendment would no longer be a crime. I think the classic example, which I will quote, of this having value is a case called *Blamar*,[416] of some years ago, where a number of road haulage contractors agreed with their drivers that the drivers should work longer hours per day than the law allowed. For a driver to exceed his hours is a summary offence, and nobody would wish it to be more, but when a large number of people combine together so that a breach of the law shall take place over a wide field we have something which, in my opinion, at any rate, requires to be touched by the criminal law in a more severe sense than the summary offence itself. The mischief of what is happening there is that a number of people are combining and thus making the result worse; and these are circumstances, I suggest, where the crime of conspiracy, which enables the combination to be the object of the attack, still has practical value.

2) 'The other example is a conspiracy to commit a trespass. Suppose that a hundred people go to a cricket match with a view to disrupting the game.... Their tactics are that as soon as the game starts two shall run out and sit on the pitch ... and after a few minutes the next two will go out, and so on. It is perfectly feasible in these circumstances for the entire game to be disrupted and for many law-abiding people who have paid their money to be deprived of their enjoyment. It is not a criminal offence of any kind to run out and sit down on the pitch, it is at worst a trespass. But surely the fact that a substantial number of people combine to do it, and thus so greatly increase the mischief of what is done, should be something which the criminal law can touch. So here again we have an example of an action which is not criminal at all but which, I suggest, is properly brought within the criminal law under the charge of conspiracy.'[417]

These are weighty objections; but there are some weighty arguments in reply:

a) Whether such conduct should be criminal is for Parliament and not for the courts to decide. If Parliament feels that certain summary offences when committed in combination present a greatly increased social danger or are more deserving of punishment, then it must provide for an aggravated punishment in the legislation penalizing the summary offence. Similarly, if Parliament feels that society in general and spectators at cricket matches in particular need protection against

[416] *Reg v Blamires Transport Services Ltd.* 1963 3 WLR 496.
[417] Hansard 24 July 1972 col 1118.

conduct of the kind witnessed in the Stop the Seventy Tour campaign (it is hard to believe that Lord Widgery had anything else in mind), then it is for Parliament to provide that protection[418] and not for private prosecutors to do so through the medium of the courts.

b) If conspiracy to trespass is to be an offence, then it is essential that there should be limits to its scope; but it is impossible in practice to find limits which can be applied with sufficient precision (this was shown in the discussion of *Kamara* in chapter 4).[419]

c) Other countries manage without an offence of conspiracy to trespass (see chapter 6).

d) The conspiracy weapon is not conceptually the neatest way of punishing acts which are done in combination, because it does not punish the acts so much as the agreement. This point was made by Lord Diplock in *Knuller*:

> 'My Lords, it may be rational to hold that there are some kinds of acts which if done by a number of people acting in concert have consequences sufficiently harmful to call for punishment by the State, but which if done by one person acting on his own have consequences that are not grave enough to demand penal sanctions. But it is the height of sophistry to say that the doing of the acts in concert which alone can have harmful consequences is not what the law regards as meriting punishment, but that the prior agreement to do them is.'[420]

e) The burden of proof, as Lady Birk pointed out in the quotation at the head of this chapter, should really be on those who wish to add offences to the criminal law rather than on those who wish to subtract from it. Lord Widgery has put forward two examples of cases which he considers should be criminal; but neither example provides sufficient justification for the propositions that all summary offences when committed in combination should be indictable, or that all trespasses committed in combination should be criminal. Proof of the need for such general propositions in our law has yet to be produced.

3) The other two objections to limiting conspiracy to agreements to commit indictable offences are that this proposal entails the disappearance of the offences of conspiracy to pervert the course of justice and conspiracy to defraud. Both these offences perform a useful function in our law and it may be desirable to retain them.

[418] Some statutory protection is already in existence. See the Conspiracy and Protection of Property Act 1875, s.7 discussed *supra* pp. 88–89.
[419] pages 52–58.
[420] 1972 3 WLR at 167.

Conspiracy to Defraud

Conspiracy to defraud was until recently (and probably still is) the most frequently employed charge of all the different heads of conspiracy. An account of the sort of cases in which the charge is found useful is provided by an article in The Cambridge Law Journal,[421] by T. B. Hadden; that article may broadly be taken as stating the case for retaining the offence. Combinations to defraud, it should be remembered, may be criminal even though the deception used would not be criminal if employed by one person alone.[422] The limits of the offence have never been judicially defined; but Hadden suggests that they are encompassed by

> 'any combination to obtain money goods or some other valuable advantage (i) without intending to give in return for it what is either reasonably expected or at least impliedly offered, or (ii) by means of some other operative false representation of fact.'[423]

In support of retaining an offence of conspiracy to defraud Hadden advances three overlapping arguments:

1) '... the charge is clearly useful in bringing to justice a significant number of persons involved in large-scale frauds who might otherwise escape prosecution'[424]

   and

   '... in the majority of cases a charge of conspiracy is felt to be the only effective means of bringing successfully executed schemes before the criminal courts. For as far as fraudulent activities are concerned the offence of conspiracy has virtually ceased to be classified as a species of attempt, and has become what can only be described as a substantive crime in its own right.'[425]

2) 'The essence of this matter in cases involving fraud lies in the desire of the prosecution to lay before the court the whole story. This is of course essential if the charge is a general one ... which relies on an overall picture of dishonesty rather than on a specific falsehood in relation to a particular transaction. In such circumstances each aspect of the accused's plan of action must be established and accounted for by the Crown as part of the fraudulent scheme: for if it is not, the defence may well be able to produce that very aspect as proof of their innocence....'[426]

[421] 1966 CLJ 248.
[422] *Warburton* 1870 11 Cox 584; *Fountain* 1966 1 WLR 212.
[423] 1966 CLJ at 255.
[424] *ibid.* at 248.
[425] *ibid.* at 259.
[426] *ibid.* at 257.

3) 'Quite apart from issues of substance however there are often very good reasons for preferring a charge of conspiracy in addition to or instead of charges of substantive offences. The most important is that the prosecution is enabled by charging a conspiracy to bring whatever evidence it chooses, within the broad limits of relevance, in respect of the whole transaction, and that the whole of this evidence will in general be admissible against each conspirator. This evidential *carte blanche* is a crucial argument in favour of retaining conspiracy to defraud as an independent offence. . . .'[427]

The following arguments may be adduced in reply:
1) There can be no good reasons for preferring a charge of conspiracy in addition to charges of substantive offences where the conspiracy count is a roll-up charge. Nor is it desirable that all the evidence introduced will in general be admissible against each conspirator; for such blanket liability leads to the results in *Griffiths*[428] and *Dawson*[429] and the other cases described above in chapter 5.[430] But quite apart from the manifest injustice which results from these blanket charges of conspiracy the charge is unnecessary because in a prosecution for the substantive offence the prosecution may introduce any evidence that is relevant; within the broad limits of relevance the prosecution should never be prevented from 'laying before the court the whole story'.
2) One of the advantages of conspiracy to defraud when Hadden wrote this article (in 1966) was that the old substantive offence of obtaining property by false pretences suffered from severe limitations, and in cases where a charge for a substantive offence was not available conspiracy to defraud provided a useful alternative. It was not limited to obtaining tangible property; and it was not limited to proving a specific falsehood, but rather relied on an overall picture of dishonesty. Since then the Theft Act 1968 has done much to remedy both these defects. In the new offence of obtaining a pecuniary advantage by deception the Act makes criminal any fraud by which D's debts are evaded or deferred or reduced, or by which he is allowed to borrow on overdraft or take out an insurance policy, or by which he is given the opportunity to get a job or win money by betting.[431] And in the interpretation of 'deception' in section 15 the Act makes a great advance on the old law of false pretences, which was limited to the false representation of an existing fact : 'deception' now means 'any deception (whether deliber-

[427] *ibid.* at 255.
[428] 1965 2 All ER 448.
[429] 1960 1 All ER 558.
[430] pp. 74–76.
[431] s.16 (2) (a) – (c). Some of these offences were covered by the old offence of obtaining credit by fraud, contrary to the Debtors Act 1869; but the scope of s.16 is much wider – see Smith, *The Law of Theft* (1968), paras. 316 and 322. S.16 has created problems of its own: see *Royle* (1971) 56 Cr App R 131 and comment thereon in 1972 Crim LR 4.

H

ate or reckless) by words or conduct as to fact or as to law, including a deception as to the present intentions of the person using the deception or any other person'.[432] This should cover most of the cases of 'falsification of others' reasonable expectations', which Hadden argued were covered by conspiracy to defraud but not by law of false pretences.

3) Nor is the Theft Act the only statutory measure which detracts from the necessity of having a general offence of conspiracy to defraud. Specific statutory offences are created by the Gaming Act 1845 (section 17); the Auctions (Bidding Agreements) Act 1927; the Prevention of Fraud (Invesments) Act 1958, and the Protection of Depositors Act 1963. Hadden himself admits:

> 'The obvious conclusion is that where it is desirable to prevent and punish particular forms of "rigging" or manipulation in the absence of either a specific misrepresentation or direct financial interest, detailed legislation is likely to be much the most effective means.'[433]

The argument for conspiracy to defraud has been based on the need for an open-ended offence to control new forms of fraudulent activity; but time and again Parliament has had to provide statutory protection – protection which is more effective because it contains detailed provisions as to what is and what is not permissible.

4) Conspiracy to defraud is a clumsy weapon because it requires the participation of more than one offender before the authorities can prosecute. Yet there is no magic in numbers; a successful fraud can be mounted by one man provided he has the skill, the organization and the plausibility.[434] It seems absurd that he should in some cases be outside the reach of the criminal law so long as he acts alone, but be liable for conspiracy to defraud as soon as he finds a partner; instead of perpetuating this anomaly it would be better to define more exactly what is and what is not fraudulent.

5) Hadden himself is no defender of the charge of conspiracy to defraud as it exists at present.

> 'The looseness of the charge and the vague state of the law in many cases of conspiracy to defraud mean that the effective decision on culpability as well as on the facts is made by the jury.'[435]

His solution is to press for a much tighter definition of the offence. But is there any need for the offence at all? The drafters of the Model

[432] Theft Act 1968, s.15 (4). For a detailed analysis of the ambit of this section, see Smith *op. cit.* paras. 243–295.

[433] *op. cit.* p. 267.

[434] For a recent expression of the orthodox view (on the greater danger of combinations) see *Fountain* 1966 1 WLR 212 (Lawton J.).

[435] *op. cit.* p. 258.

Penal Code rejected conspiracy to defraud altogether because it 'failed to provide a sufficiently definite standard of conduct;'[436] and right at the end of his article Hadden does consider the possibility of total abolition.

> 'Once this unification [*sc.* of larceny and fraud] is achieved, there will then no longer be any need for such a general, inherently undesirable and costly offence as conspiracy to defraud: its place will be taken both by the more general crime of fraudulent misappropriation, and by more detailed punitive and preventive measures.... Until the offence of conspiracy to defraud is actually abolished however there is little reason to suppose that any of these reforms will be made or even if they are made that prosecuting authorities would cease to make use of the older offence.'[437]

Hadden's 'general offence' of fraudulent misappropriation has not yet been introduced, but the Theft Act has cleared up most of the old anomalies; and the tentative conclusion must be that conspiracy to defraud no longer serves any useful purpose. This cannot be a definite conclusion without undertaking a survey of all the recent cases where conspiracy to defraud was charged, and finding out what alternative charges were available: but conceptually anyway it appears that conspiracy to defraud is rather like conspiracy to effect a public mischief – it was of use at an earlier stage of legal development, when statutory offences were not sufficiently well-developed, but it can now safely be discarded. Where no alternative charges are available (and since the passing of the Theft Act such cases will be very few), Parliament must in suitable cases create them; the creation of specific statutory offences will always provide more effective protection against the latest devices of the wickedness of man[438] (the most recent being pyramid-selling?) than a generalized offence such as conspiracy to defraud.

Conspiracy to pervert the course of justice

Rather different considerations apply with regard to conspiracy to pervert the course of justice. In the first place there is a greater need for the general offence, because there are almost no specific statutory offences controlling conduct of this kind, except for perjury and obstructing the police in the execution of their duty. In the second place the crime is one for which the conspiracy charge is particularly apposite in its proper function as an inchoate offence, because offenders are often caught only at the agreement stage – at the stage when they

[436] 1961 Columb. LR 957.
[437] 1966 CLJ at 271.
[438] See Viscount Simonds in *Shaw*, 1961 2 All ER at 452.

make an approach to a policeman or a witness or a juror – and so before they can put their plan into action.

Thirdly there is no evidence that the charge has ever been abused.[439] Some idea of the sort of conduct which it has been used to punish or prevent over the years can be gathered from the entry in Halsbury's Laws of England:

> '*Conspiracy to obstruct course of justice.* It is a misdemeanour at common law for two or more persons to conspire together to obstruct, defeat, pervert or prevent the course of public justice, either by bringing a false criminal charge against a man or by preventing a witness from giving evidence in a criminal prosecution or agreeing with him that he should not attend at the trial for that purpose, or by publishing matter calculated to interfere with the course of justice or to pervert the minds of the court or of the jurors, or by producing in court evidence known to be false, or by indemnifying bail.'[440]

All these are cases that undoubtedly should be made criminal; the only difficulty is that the limits of the offence have never been clearly defined.

It has only recently been decided that perverting the course of justice is a substantive offence in its own right. In the case of *Andrews* (1973)[441] the defendant was convicted of incitement to pervert the course of justice for offering to give false evidence at a trial in return for a sum of money; and he appealed on the ground that no substantive offence of perverting the course of justice existed. The Court of Appeal held that such an offence was known to the law, and cited two cases of attempting to pervert the course of justice in support, *Grimes* (1968)[442] and *Vreones* (1891).[443] In the latter case Lord Coleridge C.J. had said (at 366-7):

> '... I think that an attempt to pervert the course of justice is in itself a punishable misdemeanour and though I should myself have thought so on the grounds of sense and reason, there is also plenty of authority to show that it is a misdemeanour in point of law.'

Lord Widgery C.J. concluded:

> 'Accordingly, to produce false evidence with a view to misleading the court and perverting the course of public justice is a substantive

[439] Except perhaps in *Field* 1965 1 QB 404, where the possible abuse lay not in the conviction but in respect of the sentence.
[440] 10 Halsbury's Laws (3rd Edn.) 631 para. 1198.
[441] 1973 2 WLR 116.
[442] 1968 3 All ER 179.
[443] 1891 1 QB 360.

offence; an attempt so to act can be charged as such, and in our judgment an incitement so to act is also a charge known to the law. . . .'[444]

Of course this does not make it any easier to say what the limits of the offence are, and when taking an interest in the outcome of a case (*e.g.* by sowing doubts in a witness's mind) shades off into perverting the course of justice. This was substantially the point made by Wright, when after citing a dozen of the leading cases on conspiracy to pervert the course of justice, he said:

> 'On the whole it is conceived that all these are cases in which the acts proposed were, at the times when the cases were decided, punishable on indictment or information, or at least as contempts of court. But it seems possible that, in matters of this nature, the criminal courts would not hold themselves strictly bound by these limits, and that combinations for such acts on the verge of criminality might be held indictable, although the acts might not be indictable apart from the combination. It is conceived, however, that some kind of falsity or violence or abuse of process of the court would be necessary. And here the difficulty recurs of obtaining any distinct and definable limitation when once the established lines of the ordinary criminal law are overstepped.'[445]

This is substantially the position today. Even if perverting the course of justice is a common law offence, conspiracy to pervert the course of justice is not necessarily limited to the confines of that offence; but anyway since the limits of the substantive offence are so undefined it makes little difference in practice. No one doubts that conduct intended to undermine the course of justice should be made criminal, and conspiracy to pervert the courst of justice is a useful offence to that end. What is needed is some detailed definition by the legislature of what sort of conduct constitutes the offence – of exactly what is and what is not permissible (similar provisions are even more necessary with regard to the offence of contempt of court). Otherwise decisions by the courts, however right, smack strongly of *ex post facto* legislation. Justice according to law demands that judges are not free to hand down decisions based purely on their own ideas of what is just, no matter how good and wise those decisions may be; there should be a fixed standard by which citizens may shape their conduct and by which justice can be reasonably foreseen. Conspiring to pervert the course of

[444] 1973 2 WLR at 119.
[445] *op. cit.* p. 31.

justice should be retained; but the details of what constitutes the offence should be more closely defined.

Conclusions

It remains to consider whether Lady Birk's amendment is a sufficient reform of the law. At the very least conspiracy should be limited to indictable offences; but should we go further than that? It has been suggested that if we are to have a crime of conspiracy at all, it should not be an across-the-board inchoate offence, but rather that it should apply to a limited number of specified indictable offences, and not to others. For example (taking some crimes at random) it should be criminal to conspire to rob or commit bigamy, but not be criminal to conspire to rape or commit forgery. The difficulty with this proposal is that it is impossible to formulate any relevant criteria as a basis for selecting those offences in respect of which one can commit conspiracy, and those in respect of which one cannot. The gravity of the offence is no longer a relevant consideration once conspiracy has been limited to indictable offences (summary offences having been excluded on the principle *de minimis non curat lex*); and any other selection will be purely arbitrary, since this really is a case where 'no one can foresee every way in which the wickedness of man may disrupt the order of society'.[446] If it is thought necessary to keep conspiracy for some indictable offences, then it must be kept in respect of them all.

In one respect Lady Birk's amendment is insufficient, and that is that it does not attempt to offer a new *definition* of the crime of conspiracy; it merely seeks to restrict the scope of the crime. In making no attempt to define what is meant by 'conspire' or 'conspiracy', it does not solve any of the technical problems which arise from imputing criminality to a mere agreeement. Here a unilateral definition of the crime, such as the one provided by the American Penal Code,[447] would be a great improvement; and specification of the *mens rea* required in conspiracy would provide a limitation of liability for those who are only peripherally involved.

[446] *per* Viscount Simonds in *Shaw*, 1961 2 All ER at 452.
[447] see chapter 8 *supra*, pp. 103–4.

10. PROPOSALS FOR REFORM: PROCEDURE

I. *Roll-up charges*

It is evident that judicial protests have not succeeded in stopping this practice, and something more is required. The common law rule used to be that the conspiracy merged into the felony if the felony was committed; but this rule was abandoned in *Button* (1848).[448] If the doctrine of merger were revived it would prevent the prosecution from charging a defendant with conspiracy where the substantive offence had been completed. However there may be cases of large-scale crime (*e.g.* the Great Train Robbery) where a prosecution for conspiracy is appropriate because it enables the prosecution to lay before the court an overall picture of the scheme; but in such cases there should be a *prima facie* rule that the conspiracy charge be tried separately from any other offences. This procedure has already been suggested by the Court of Criminal Appeal:

> 'In our judgment, except in simple cases, a conspiracy count (if one is needed at all) should be tried separately to substantive counts.' (Paull J. in *Griffiths*)[449]

Proof of conspiracy is substantially different from proof of other offences; and if in every case there was a right to separate trial on a conspiracy count (which the prosecution could oppose by showing that there would be no prejudice to the defendant), then prosecutors would be more sparing in their use of conspiracy charges when drafting indictments.

II. *The drafting of the Indictment*

There are two abuses here which need to be altered. The first relates to the giving of particulars of the offence. At the moment this is simply

[448] 11 QB 929.
[449] 1965 2 All ER at 250.

a beneficial practice which the trial judge may direct at his discretion; but the giving of particulars should be something for which the defence can apply as of right.

Of course in the vast majority of cases the prosecution do provide sufficient particulars; but this is no reason why they should not be made to do so in all cases. Most of the cases reported on this point have in fact been trials for conspiracy to defraud; but even if conspiracy to defraud is done away with the problems will remain. Under the present law if two defendants are indicted for a statutory offence, particulars of the offence must be given in the indictment; but if they are indicted for conspiracy to commit it, the indictment is good if it merely follows the words of the statute (*Rowlands*).[450]

This is highly unsatisfactory. The prosecution should be obliged to settle in advance the particular acts which are to be relied upon; this will not only prevent possible abuse, but it will serve to pinpoint the issues before the court, and will make it easier to exclude evidence which does not bear directly on those issues. This in its turn will make the trial of complicated cases simpler, quicker and cheaper.

The second abuse is related to the first. It is the practice of charging a defendant of conspiring 'with others unknown' where the others are perfectly well known to the prosecution. There may be good reasons why all the alleged conspirators cannot be charged together; but at least where the others are known the prosecution should name them in the indictment. Indeed, this would seem to be the corollary of Rule 8 of the Indictment Rules 1971, which states: 'It shall be sufficient in an indictment to describe a person whose name is not known as a person unknown'. It follows that a person whose name *is* known should be described by that name. Otherwise an already nebulous charge becomes even more nebulous.

There is already some very slight authority for such a procedure. In *Oswin*[451] the defendant was convicted on a charge that over a period of 16 months he conspired with others unknown to publish certain obscene articles. The prosecution explained that the unknown persons were the suppliers of the articles and the prospective purchasers; but the Court of Criminal Appeal held the count bad for vagueness and uncertainty, one of the (admittedly subsidiary) reasons being that no fellow conspirator was named.

In civil law one cannot allege the existence of an oral contract without showing with whom the agreement is made; the rule should be no less strict in criminal law. In the first Angry Brigade trial the prosecution perfectly properly charged Prescott and Purdie with conspiring with eight other named persons (those who subsequently

[450] 1851 17 QB 671.
[451] 1964 Crim LR 479.

became known as the Stoke Newington Eight), but Peter Hain was charged with conspiring with others unknown, when the other organizers of his campaign were perfectly well known. In such cases the prosecution should supply the names of the alleged co-conspirators as a material part of the particulars.

III. *The Hearsay Rule*

The justification sometimes advanced for excluding the rule against hearsay evidence in conspiracy trials is that conspiracy tends to be a clandestine offence, and the prosecution in most cases will be unable to prove the existence of an agreement by direct evidence. There are however certain cases (usually of a quasi-political kind) where the agreement is a *public* one, or where the defendants made no attempt to conceal its existence: examples would be the cases of *Oz* and *IT*, and the trial of *Spock* in the United States (in which 5 leaders of the anti-war movement were charged with conspiring to counsel, aid and abet young men to avoid the draft). In these cases there is no reason why the rules of evidence, relaxed in the average conspiracy case merely to facilitate proof of the agreement, should not be raised to their normal standard.

In the normal conspiracy case it is extremely difficult to say what alterations can be made to the rules of evidence to minimize the prejudicial effects of a conspiracy trial. Hadden has suggested that all evidence should be admissible against everybody:

> 'The most acceptable solution to this point would seem to be to provide that in any joint indictment, whether involving a conspiracy charge or not, the acts of any person involved should be admitted in evidence to assist the jury to decide upon the guilt or innocence of each party. The interests of justice will surely be better served by admitting all relevant evidence than by interminable disputes as to what is and what is not admissible against this or that party; and those of the accused should be adequately protected by their right to apply to the judge for a separate trial. . . . The correct result is more likely to be achieved as a result of competent directions and summing up by the judge on the extent of the evidence against each party and the taking of a separate verdict for each of the defendants than by confusing the jury with detailed instructions as to what they must pretend not to have heard in respect of each party.'[452]

This proposal has a strong common-sense appeal, but it is too sweeping to work well in practice. Some evidence must still be inadmissible, as being hopelessly prejudicial to one or more of the defendants; and the right to separate trial is not an adequate safeguard. Separate trials

[452] 1966 CLJ at 268.

are very rarely granted, and quite properly not; where defendants are charged with a joint offence they should wherever possible be tried jointly – this will enable the jury to hear the whole story, both time and money will be saved thereby, and inconsistent verdicts avoided. The second drawback of Hadden's proposal is that it places an intolerable strain on the judge if he has to put off the decision (in effect) as to what is and what is not admissible until his summing-up speech; and if the judge does not direct the jury on the extent of the evidence against each defendant then it puts an intolerable strain on the jury.

Perhaps the problem is best approached from an altogether different angle, by asking who is most likely to suffer injustice as a result of a conspiracy trial. The real victims of conspiracy procedure are defendants facing a roll-up charge who should properly have been charged with a substantive offence; and defendants who should never have been in the dock at all because their involvement in the whole business is essentially peripheral. If these people are charged with a substantive offence, or not charged at all because they lack the requisite degree of *mens rea*, then the problems relating to the admissibility of evidence in a conspiracy trial should be no different from those in an ordinary joint trial (as Glanville Williams has pointed out);[453] and they should be approached from this point of view. It is interesting to note in this context (without comment) the proposal of the Criminal Law Revision Committee's Eleventh Report, on Evidence,[454] that the prosecution should be able to give in evidence against one defendant a statement made by another defendant jointly tried with him.[455] If the proposal of the Committee 'to admit all hearsay evidence likely to be valuable to the greatest extent possible'[456] is accepted, then the difference between the rules of evidence in a conspiracy case and a normal trial will largely disappear.

IV. *Presentation of the Defence*

In a complex trial the individual defence lawyer seldom defends his client against the whole conspiracy charge, but merely against those elements in which his client appears to have been involved. As a result the jury never hears a general defence to the general charge; and the suggestion has been made in America[457] that in such a case there should be 'co-ordinating' defence counsel who can advise with respect to those areas in which the interests of all the defendants are the same.

However the case for such counsel has not been sufficiently made out

[453] *op. cit.* p. 684.
[454] July 1972 Cmnd. 4991.
[455] *ibid.* paras 236 and 251.
[456] *ibid.* para 238.
[457] Wessel in 38 Notre Dame Lawyer 689.

to justify recommending it here. To have common defence counsel would be most undesirable because of the difficulty of representing conflicting interests; the co-ordinating counsel must be supplementary to individual defendants' counsel. But it is difficult to see what co-ordinating counsel can do that the other defending counsel do not at the moment arrange, informally, between themselves to do; there is sufficient co-ordination of the defence in English conspiracy trials, without it being necessary to present a general defence to the general charge.

It is essential that the evidence against different defendants should be kept separate in the jury's mind; to this end the practice[458] adopted in *Newland* or that used in the second *Angry Brigade* trial should become standard.

V. *Sentencing*

Where defendants are convicted of conspiracy to commit a substantive offence, it should be a rule of law that the sentence should not be greater than the maximum which could be passed for the substantive offence. This was the effect of Lady Birk's Amendment 37(2).[459] It follows as a logical conclusion from reducing conspiracy to its proper function as an inchoate offence: the sentence for attempt cannot be greater than that for the completed offence – nor should that for conspiracy. The only justification for passing a heavier sentence for conspiracy is the general danger rationale, discussed above (and rejected) in chapter 7.

[458] *supra* pp. 81–82.
[459] see p. 109.

11 SUMMARY OF MAIN CONCLUSIONS

1. No significant reform of the law of conspiracy can now be achieved except by legislation: pages 106–8.
2. Before any 'reform' of the present crime is recommended, consideration should be given to the possibility of abolishing conspiracy altogether: pages 108–9.
3. If conspiracy is retained, it should be limited to agreements to commit crimes, *i.e.*

   a) Conspiracy to commit any tort should be abolished: pages 51–8 and 110–11.
   b) Conspiracy to effect a public mischief should be abolished: pages 69–72.
   c) Conspiracy to corrupt public morals should be abolished: pages 59–69.
   d) Conspiracy to outrage public decency should be abolished: pages 68–9.
   e) Conspiracy to defraud should be abolished: pages 112–15.
   f) Conspiracy to pervert the course of justice should be retained: pages 115–18.

4. Conspiracy to commit a crime should be limited to agreements to commit indictable offences: pages 50–1 and 109–11.
5. Roll-up charges should be automatically struck out of any indictment: pages 73–8 and 119.
6. Where a conspiracy count is properly included, there should be a *prima facie* right to a separate trial on that count: page 119.
7. A sentence passed for conspiracy should never exceed the maximum which can be imposed for the substantive offence: pages 95–7 and 123.

12. POSTCRIPT

The law of criminal conspiracy is at the moment going through a period of very rapid change. Nine conspiracy cases have gone to the House of Lords in the last 15 years,[460] and at the time of writing *Hain* is about to go before the Court of Appeal.[460a] Because the law is in such a state of flux, it has been extremely difficult to write about it with any degree of certainty; for this reason wherever possible the words of the judges themselves have been used – which has revealed several sharp conflicts of judicial opinion, but which also has meant that much of the present law has stood condemned by the very people who declare it.

One consequence of all this appellate activity is that much of the law is becoming more certain. We do know now for certain that there is an offence of conspiracy to corrupt public morals, and that there is an offence of conspiracy to outrage public decency; and in 1973 when *Kamara* went to the House of Lords we learnt that not all agreements to commit torts are criminal, but only those which fall into two broadly-defined categories. But this is *not* to say that the *scope* of the law is becoming more certain; the categories of conspiracy may become more certain while the classes of behaviour which they cover remain equally vague.

And indeed this is the case. There is undoubtedly an offence of conspiracy to effect a public mischief, but as to what constitutes a public mischief only a judge can say.[461] There is an offence of conspiracy to corrupt public morals, but as to what constitutes corruption only a jury can decide;[462] bearing in mind of course that 'corrupt' is a

[460] *B.o.T. v Owen* (1957); *Shaw v DPP* (1961); *Chandler v DPP* (1962); *Churchill v Walton* (1967); *Verrier v DPP* (1967); *Bhagwan* (1970); *Knuller* (1972); *Doot* (1973); *Kamara* (1973).

[460a] By March 1974 two more appeals to the Lords had been announced: *Withers* 1974 2 WLR 26 (conspiracy to effect a public mischief) and *Scott* Times Law Report January 29 1974 (conspiracy to defraud).

[461] *Kamara* and *Porter* 1910 1 KB 369. This makes nonsense of the argument of the House of Lords in *Shaw* that arbitrary decisions will be avoided by the good sense of juries: the public mischief question is not left for the jury to decide. But see *Foy* 1972 Crim LR 504, upholding *Porter* and distinguishing *Shaw* as a public morals case.

[462] This is no longer certain in the light of the House of Lords' decision in *Kamara*, which included *Shaw* in its list of public mischief cases: what is corrupting *may* now be a question of law for the judge.

strong word.[463] And finally there is the offence of conspiracy to outrage public decency, but as to what constitutes such an offence once again only a jury can decide (bearing in mind that 'outrage' is also a strong word, and that recognized minimum standards of decency vary from time to time).[464] The inevitable conclusion is that the conduct which *might* be criminal as a result of these offences covers a far wider field than the relatively small class of acts which we know from past decisions actually to be criminal.

This is the main evil of the present law. It cannot seriously be argued that the third head of conspiracy has been used to convict a significant number of people who otherwise would have gone free. In all the reported public mischief cases an alternative charge was available, the vast majority being conspiracies to commit a crime. In the unreported cases it is impossible to say how many of the defendants could have been charged with alternative offences; certainly not all of them, but probably more than half. As for conspiracy to corrupt public morals, *Shaw* was convicted of offences under the Obscene Publications Act and the Sexual Offences Act (living on immoral earnings) as well as being found guilty of conspiracy; the 30 prosecutions of blue films following *Shaw* could have been brought for the common law misdemeanour of conducting an obscene or indecent public exhibition;[465] and the defendants in *Knuller* could have been prosecuted for procuring under s.4 of the Sexual Offences Act 1967, or for inciting the statutory offence of doing acts of gross indecency with males under the age of 21. But if they were to be found guilty of those offences they were entitled to be charged with them, and to have the verdict of a jury properly instructed by a judge upon the legal character of those particular crimes.

Kamara is in a class of its own, since it may give rise to an extension of the scope of conspiracy which will be every bit as serious as the landmark decision in *Shaw*. But here again the conspiracy charge was not necessary to obtain a conviction, for the students were also guilty of unlawful assembly, and their appeal on this count was on strictly technical grounds, which failed. It is impossible to predict what use prosecutors (both public and private) will make of this new offence; but the prosecution for conspiracy to trespass of the building workers' demonstration in Birmingham (reported on page 91) is not a good sign.

What is most disturbing of all among the recent developments in conspiracy has been its increasing use as a charge in political or quasi-political trials. It has been used to attack the Underground and the advocates of an alternative society in the trials of *Oz* and *IT*, and the first and second trials of the Angry Brigade. It has been used to attack

[463] *Per* Lord Reid in *Knuller* 1972 3 WLR at 148.
[464] *Per* Lord Simon of Glaisdale in *Knuller, ibid* at 184.
[465] according to Lord Diplock in *Knuller,* 1972 3 WLR at 171.

the revolutionary Irish in the trial of *de Faoit and others*, the *Aldershot bomb* trial, the *Old Bailey bomb* trial and several more. It has been used as a weapon against demonstrators in the prosecutions of *Chandler* and *Hain* and *Kamara*. And most recently it has been used once again against trade unionists in the trials of the Shrewsbury and the Birmingham building workers. One of the standard criminal law text books, Russell on Crime, opens its section on Conspiracy with the words:

> 'The crime of conspiracy affords support for any who advance the proposition that the criminal law is an instrument of government.'

These words are beginning to look dangerously true.

13. INDEX OF CASES

Cases are listed under the name of the accused whenever the usual method of citation would cause them to be preceded by the abbreviation '*R. v.*' or '*D.P.P. v.*'.